30 days DRAWING ANIME LIKE AN ARTIST FOR KIDS

OF_____

MW00892140

© Copyright 2023 - All rights reserved.

The content contained in this book is protected by copyright law and may not be reproduced, copied, or transmitted without explicit written consent from the author or the publisher.

The publisher and the author shall not be held responsible or legally liable for any damage, compensation, or financial loss resulting from the information presented in this book, whether directly or indirectly.

Legal Notice:

This book is copyrighted and intended for personal use only. Any alteration, distribution, sale, use, quotation, or paraphrasing of any part or content from this book is strictly prohibited without permission from the author or publisher.

Disclaimer Notice:

Please note that the information provided in this document is intended solely for educational and entertainment purposes. Every effort has been made to offer accurate, up-to-date, reliable, and comprehensive information. No guarantees, either express or implied, are made. Readers acknowledge that the author is not providing legal, financial, medical, or professional advice. The content in this book has been gathered from various sources. It is advisable to consult a licensed professional before attempting any techniques mentioned in this book.

By reading this document, the reader agrees that the author cannot be held responsible, under any circumstances, for any losses, whether direct or indirect, incurred as a result of using the information provided in this document. This includes, but is not limited to, errors, omissions, or inaccuracies.

Patricia Rogers

Patricia Rogers, a prominent figure in the realm of anime artistry, is renowned for her exceptional talent in crafting engaging anime and manga illustrations targeted specifically at children. Born and raised in the vibrant landscapes of America, Patricia discovered her passion for art at a young age, finding inspiration in the colorful world of anime.

At the age of 38, Patricia has established herself as a distinguished artist and author, captivating young audiences with her unique approach to teaching the art of drawing anime and manga. Her creative journey has led her to author several instructive books tailored for children, aiming to nurture budding artists and ignite their passion for the captivating realm of anime.

With a keen eye for detail and a profound understanding of the nuances of anime aesthetics, Patricia's artwork resonates with readers, bringing to life vibrant characters and enchanting narratives. Her dedication to the art form is evident in the intricate brushstrokes and vivid colors that grace the pages of her creations.

In addition to her artistic pursuits, Patricia is a fervent advocate for art education in schools, believing in the transformative power of creativity in shaping young minds. Through workshops, school visits, and online tutorials, she shares her knowledge and expertise, inspiring countless aspiring artists to explore the boundless possibilities of anime art.

Despite her achievements, Patricia remains humble and deeply passionate about her craft. Her commitment to empowering the next generation of artists continues to drive her artistic endeavors, making her a beloved figure in the world of anime and manga.

Patricia Rogers stands as a testament to the limitless potential of creativity and remains a guiding light for young artists, inspiring them to dream big and explore the endless horizons of anime art.

WHAT YOU NEED

Imagine you want to play guitar like a famous rock star. Having the coolest, most expensive guitar won't magically turn you into a guitar hero, right? Well, the same goes for art! Some young artists worry about having the fanciest art supplies, thinking it'll make them draw like a professional artist. But here's the secret: it's not about the tools, it's about how you use them and how creative you can get. Just like finding your perfect guitar style takes practice and trying different guitars, discovering your art style comes from experimenting with different pencils, brands, and techniques. So, don't be afraid to explore! Your creativity is the real magic ingredient when you're drawing anime!

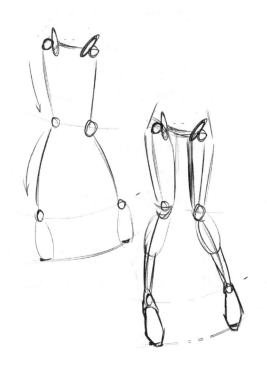

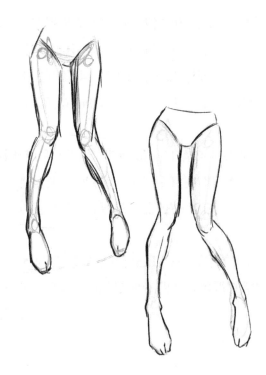

PAPER

IT'S HEART-WRENCHING TO SEE SOMEONE POUR THEIR HEART AND SOUL INTO A DRAWING, ONLY TO FIND IT ON A FLIMSY PIECE OF NOTEBOOK PAPER. HERE'S A GOLDEN TIP: INVEST IN A BRISTOL SMOOTH DRAWING PAPER PAD! IT'S LIKE UPGRADING FROM A BIKE TO A SLEEK MOTORCYCLE. THIS PAPER IS THICK AND ROBUST, PERFECT FOR ALL YOUR ARTISTIC ADVENTURES. IT CAN HANDLE ALL THE ERASING AND REDRAWING YOU THROW AT IT WITHOUT BREAKING A SWEAT. IMAGINE IT AS THE PERFECT CANVAS THAT MAKES YOUR DRAWINGS SHINE BRIGHTER AND SMOOTHER. SO, WHY SETTLE FOR A BUMPY ROAD WHEN YOU CAN CRUISE ON A SMOOTH HIGHWAY OF CREATIVITY?

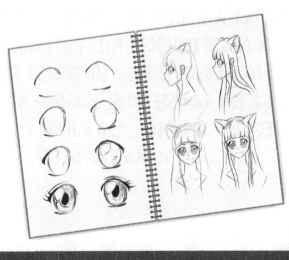

PENCILS, PENS, RULERS

Choosing your art tools is like picking your favorite ice cream flavor - it's all about what feels right for you! Pencils come in different types - some are harder, and some are softer. But watch out, the softer ones can smudge more easily. The first things to consider are how hard the pencil is and its quality. Personally, I like using a regular No. 2 pencil, but you should try a bunch to find what feels perfect in your hand. Your pencil should be your buddy, fitting just right and not getting dull or messy over time.

Now, let's talk about pens! Art stores have a bunch of cool pens you can choose from. Each pen tip creates a different line, so don't limit yourself to super thin lines. Instead, get a variety of pens with different tip widths - it's like having a whole team of superheroes with different powers! And hey, for those long lines, a 15-inch ruler is your superhero tool. Make sure it's transparent plastic so you can see your drawing while you work. Now, armed with your perfect pencils, pens, and ruler, you're ready to create your artistic masterpieces!

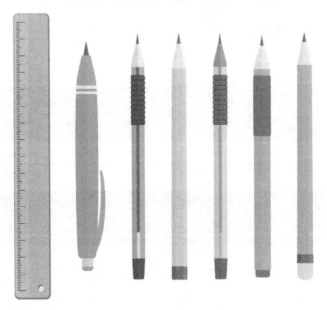

PENCIL SHARPENERS, ERASERS

Let's talk about some cool tools to make your drawings awesome! First up, pencil sharpeners. You know what? The simple handheld sharpeners you find at school or in your art kit work better than those fancy electric ones. They keep your pencils sharp and are super easy to use - just like sharpening a sword before a big adventure!

Now, onto kneaded erasers! These are like magic erasers for artists. Need to erase a big area? Kneaded erasers are your superheroes! You can find them at art stores. They're big, soft, and leave way less pink dust on your paper. Sure, they might not always be super precise, but here's a trick: use a smaller pencil eraser along with them, and you'll have the perfect team to erase anything you want in your drawings!

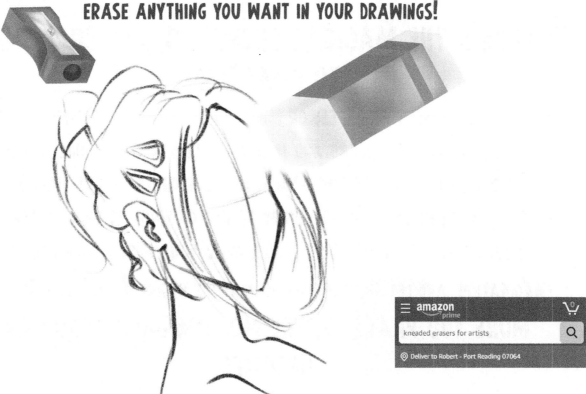

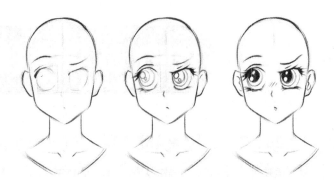

HEY THERE, YOUNG ARTIST! REMEMBER, YOU'VE GOT THE POWER WITHIN YOU! BELIEVE IN YOURSELF BECAUSE YOU CAN ABSOLUTELY DO THIS! DRAWING ANIME MIGHT SEEM LIKE A BIG ADVENTURE, BUT WITH EVERY STROKE, YOU'RE CREATING A WORLD FULL OF MAGIC AND WONDER. SO, PUT ON YOUR CREATIVE CAPE AND DIVE IN! AND GUESS WHAT? ALONG THE WAY, YOU'LL COLLECT TONS OF GOOD VIBES AND HAPPY FEELINGS. LET YOUR IMAGINATION SOAR, AND WHO KNOWS WHAT AMAZING ANIME CHARACTERS AND STORIES YOU'LL BRING TO LIFE!

SO HERE'S THE MAGICAL SECRET: IT ALL COMES DOWN TO PRACTICE!

JUST LIKE LEARNING A NEW SPELL OR MASTERING A GAME, PRACTICING YOUR ART SKILLS IS LIKE WAVING A WAND AND MAKING YOUR DRAWINGS COME ALIVE! WITH EACH DOODLE AND SKETCH, YOU'RE UNLOCKING THE SECRETS OF ART. IMAGINE IT LIKE GOING ON A THRILLING QUEST WHERE EVERY STROKE OF YOUR PENCIL IS A STEP CLOSER TO BECOMING A TRUE ART WIZARD. SO, GRAB YOUR PENCILS, GATHER YOUR IMAGINATION, AND LET THE CREATIVE ADVENTURE BEGIN! REMEMBER, THE MORE YOU PRACTICE, THE MORE MAGICAL YOUR ART BECOMES!

HERE'S THE KEY: NEVER GIVE UP! THE REAL
MAGIC HAPPENS WHEN YOU PRACTICE
DRAWING A LOT! IT'S LIKE PLANTING SEEDS IN
A MAGICAL GARDEN. THE MORE YOU DRAW,
THE MORE YOUR SKILLS GROW, JUST LIKE
FLOWERS BLOOMING IN SPRING. SO, KEEP
GOING, BE PATIENT, AND BELIEVE IN YOURSELF.
BEFORE YOU KNOW IT, YOU'LL SEE YOUR ART
SKILLS REACHING FOR THE STARS!

CROSSHATCHING

Picture this: using a special technique called crosshatching can transform your drawing into a masterpiece! It's like adding a sprinkle of magic to your artwork. The key trick? Pay attention to the spaces between your lines - that's what makes it really awesome! Just like connecting the dots in a puzzle, these lines come together to create something truly amazing. So, grab your pencils and let the crosshatching adventure begin! Your drawings will shine brighter than ever!

CROSSHATCHING DRAWING

MASTERING THE ART OF CROSS-HATCHING MIGHT SOUND TRICKY, BUT IT'S NOT AS HARD AS IT SEEMS. THERE ARE A FEW KEY THINGS YOU NEED TO KNOW TO GET IT RIGHT:

HAVE CONFIDENCE IN YOURSELF! DON'T FEAR MAKING MISTAKES - IT'S OKAY TO BE WRONG SOMETIMES!

CONSISTENT PRACTICE IS THE KEY! MAKE IT A HABIT TO DRAW FOR AT LEAST AN HOUR EVERY DAY, AND WITHIN A MONTH, YOU'LL SEE INCREDIBLE PROGRESS!

UNLOCK YOUR FULL POTENTIAL! INVEST YOUR TIME IN MASTERING COMPLEX OBJECTS BY FIRST PERFECTING SIMPLE ONES. THE FOUNDATION OF INTRICATE DRAWINGS LIES IN MASTERING THE BASICS!

SMOOTH HAND MOVEMENTS ARE KEY! YOU DON'T NEED TO PRESS TOO HARD WITH THE PENCIL. GENTLE STROKES ON THE PAPER WILL GIVE YOU THE PERFECT OUTCOME

CROSSHATCHING VARIETIES

- BASIC CROSSHATCHING
- ADDITIONAL CROSSHATCHING
- COMPLEX TYPES OF CROSSHATCHING

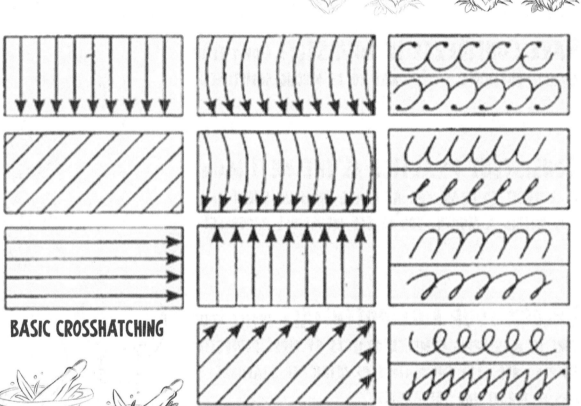

BASIC CROSSHATCHING

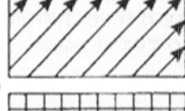

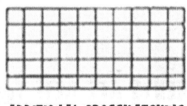

ADDITIONAL CROSSHATCHING

COMPLEX TYPES OF CROSSHATCHING

SKETCH HATCHING

Get ready for a cool journey into the world of shading with pencils! I'm going to show you some awesome shading styles and the right way to make those hatches. It's like adding magic shadows to your drawings - are you excited to learn the secrets?

TRAIN YOUR SKILLS

1. Take a deep breath and chill out!
2. Let your hand loosen up, like it's dancing!
3. Ready to follow my awesome art guide?

Activity 1: Start by drawing with the lightest touch, as if your pencil is floating on air. Then, give it another go and see your drawing come to life!

TRAIN YOUR SKILLS

HEY THERE, SUPER ARTISTS! DON'T STRESS IF THINGS DON'T GO
PERFECTLY ON YOUR FIRST TRY! MISTAKES ARE JUST DETOURS
ON THE CREATIVE ADVENTURE!

TIP: REPEAT THIS ACTIVITY FOR A FEW DAYS! IT'S A GOOD IDEA TO HAVE A
SPECIAL WORKBOOK WHERE YOU CAN PRACTICE THESE EXERCISES. THINK OF IT AS
YOUR MAGICAL ART JOURNAL!

TRAIN YOUR DRAWING SKILLS

SKETCH HATCHING MAGIC: YOU MIGHT THINK THIS ACTIVITY SOUNDS DULL AT FIRST, BUT WAIT UNTIL I SPRINKLE SOME EXCITEMENT INTO IT! MANY FOLKS OVERLOOK ITS IMPORTANCE, BUT TOGETHER, WE'LL TURN THIS EXERCISE INTO A SUPER FUN AND UNIQUE ADVENTURE!

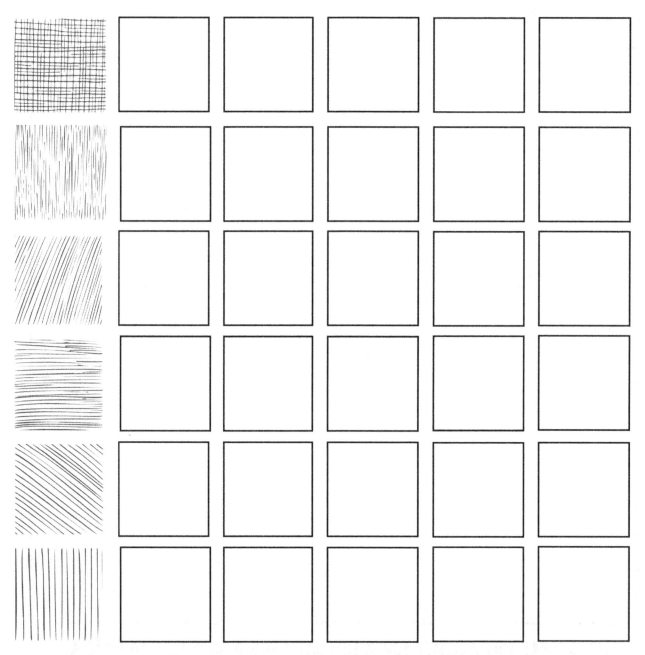

IMAGINE A MAGICAL SKETCHBOOK WHERE YOU CAN BRING YOUR CREATIVE IDEAS TO LIFE!

TRAIN YOUR DRAWING SKILLS

TRAIN YOUR DRAWING SKILLS

TRAIN YOUR DRAWING SKILLS

TRAIN YOUR DRAWING SKILLS

TRAIN HAND MOTOR SKILLS

EXPLORE THE WORLD OF ROUND SHAPES!

DIVING INTO THE WORLD OF ROUND SHAPES CAN BE A SUPER FUN ADVENTURE FOR BUDDING ARTISTS LIKE YOU! WHY, YOU ASK? WELL, PRACTICING PATTERNS WITH ROUND SHAPES ISN'T JUST A CREATIVE EXERCISE; IT'S LIKE A MAGICAL KEY THAT UNLOCKS YOUR ARTISTIC ABILITIES.

THE COOLEST PART? AS YOU KEEP DRAWING THOSE ROUND SHAPES, YOUR HAND BECOMES FRIENDS WITH THE PENCIL, MAKING YOU THE MASTER OF YOUR ART TOOLS. IT'S LIKE TRAINING FOR A BIG ART ADVENTURE! AND GUESS WHAT? THESE ROUND PATTERNS AREN'T JUST DOTS ON A PAGE; THEY ADD A SPRINKLE OF MAGIC TO YOUR ARTWORK. THEY CREATE DEPTH, MAKING YOUR DRAWINGS POP WITH EXCITEMENT AND ENERGY.

TRAIN HAND MOTOR SKILLS

So, LET YOUR IMAGINATION SOAR AS YOU EXPLORE THE ENDLESS WORLD OF ROUND SHAPES! WITH EVERY CIRCLE, YOU'RE NOT JUST DRAWING; YOU'RE BUILDING A MASTERPIECE, ONE CURVE AT A TIME. LET THE FUN AND CREATIVITY FLOW!

TRAIN HAND MOTOR SKILLS

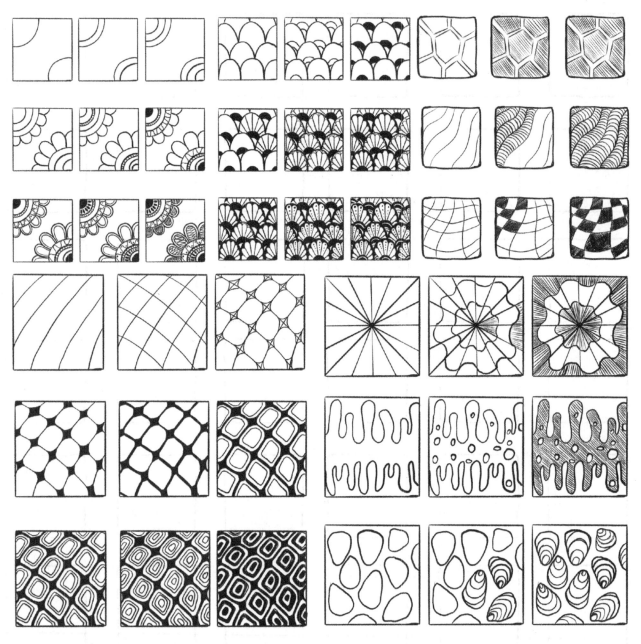

IMAGINE THIS: EVERY TIME YOU DRAW A ROUND SHAPE, YOU'RE NOT JUST MAKING A CIRCLE; YOU'RE BUILDING YOUR UNDERSTANDING OF SHAPES AND FORMS. IT'S LIKE CONNECTING THE DOTS OF CREATIVITY! PLUS, PLAYING AROUND WITH THESE ORGANIC, FLOWING LINES ISN'T JUST ABOUT DRAWING; IT'S ABOUT DANCING YOUR PENCIL ON THE PAPER, CREATING PATTERNS THAT COME TO LIFE.

TRAIN HAND MOTOR SKILLS

BASICS OF SHADING

OBSERVE HOW THE LEVELS ON THE VALUE SCALE CORRESPOND TO THE SHADING IN THE DRAWING.

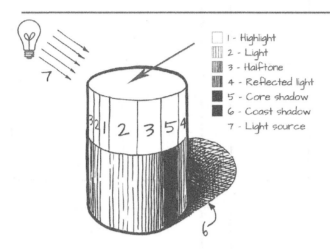

1 - Highlight
2 - Light
3 - Halftone
4 - Reflected light
5 - Core shadow
6 - Coast shadow
7 - Light source

IDENTIFY YOUR **LIGHT SOURCE**. WHERE THE LIGHT HITS YOUR OBJECT WILL BE THE **HIGHLIGHT** OR THE LIGHTEST **VALUE**.

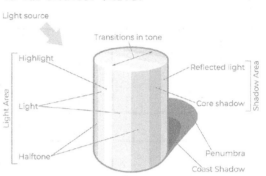

Light source

Transitions in tone

Highlight

Light Area

Light

Halftone

Reflected light

Core shadow

Shadow Area

Penumbra

Coast Shadow

5 WAYS TO SHADE:
1. STIPPLE 2. HATCH 3. CROS SHATCH
4. SCRIBBLE 5. BLEND

1. STIPPLE
USE SMALL DOTS TO CREATE **VALUE**.

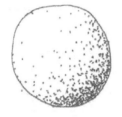

2. HATCH
USE PARALLEL LINES TO CREATE **VALUE**.

3. CROSS HATCH
USE CROSSING LINES TO CREATE **VALUE**.

4. SCRIBBLE
USE LOOPED, CROSSED, SCRIBBLE LINES TO CREATE **VALUE**.

5. BLEND
COLOR IN THE SHADOW, THEN SMOOTH IT OUT TO CREATE **VALUE**.

VALUE SCALE:
SHOWS THE RANGE FROM THE DARKEST VALUES TO THE LIGHTEST VALUES IN EVEN STEPS.

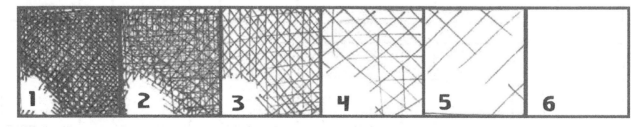

1   2   3   4   5   6

26

TRAIN SHADING SKILLS

Experiment with five different shading techniques provided below. Utilize the arrows as a reference for the direction of the light source, guiding you on where to place highlights and shadows.

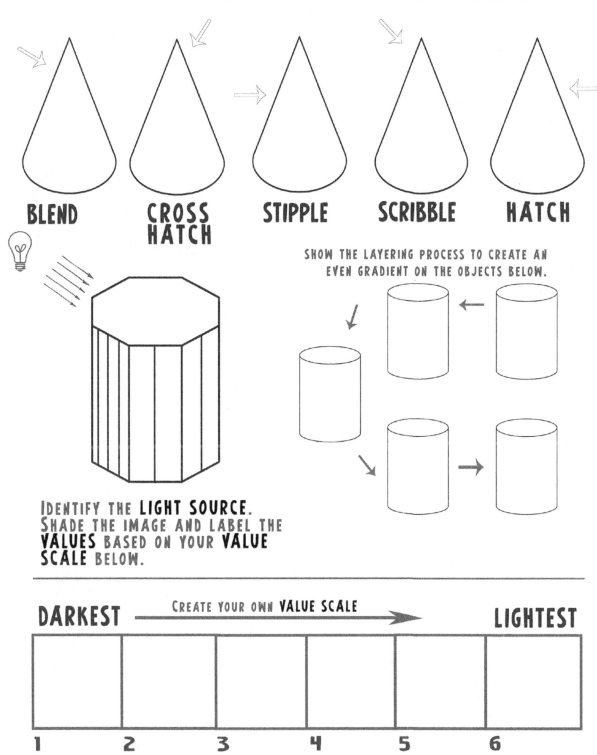

BLEND   CROSS HATCH   STIPPLE   SCRIBBLE   HATCH

SHOW THE LAYERING PROCESS TO CREATE AN EVEN GRADIENT ON THE OBJECTS BELOW.

IDENTIFY THE **LIGHT SOURCE.** SHADE THE IMAGE AND LABEL THE **VALUES** BASED ON YOUR **VALUE SCALE** BELOW.

DARKEST ——— CREATE YOUR OWN **VALUE SCALE** ———→ LIGHTEST

1	2	3	4	5	6

TRAIN SHADING SKILLS

REPEAT AS ABOVE!

1. STIPPLE
USE SMALL DOTS
TO CREATE **VALUE.**

TRAIN SHADING SKILLS

2.HATCH
USE PARALLEL LINES TO
CREATE VALUE.

3.CROSS HATCH
USE CROSSING LINES TO
CREATE VALUE. VALUE.

TRAIN SHADING SKILLS

4. SCRIBBLE
USE LOOPED, CROSSED, SCRIBBLE LINES TO CREATE **VALUE.**

5. BLEND
COLOR IN THE SHADOW, THEN SMOOTH IT OUT TO CREATE **VALUE.**

TRAIN SHADING SKILLS

TRAIN SHADING SKILLS

Levek UP!

LET'S TALK ABOUT GEOMETRIC SHAPES!

Geometric shapes might sound simple, but they are the building blocks of art and design. Imagine circles, squares, triangles, rectangles, and ovals - these are the superheroes of art! When you learn to play with these basic shapes, you unlock a world of creative possibilities.

For budding artists like you, mastering these shapes is like getting the keys to an artist's toolbox. They help you understand cool techniques like perspective, shading, and how to arrange things on your canvas. You see, drawing these shapes isn't just about lines and curves; it's about grasping the secrets of form, space, and

But here's the exciting part: these shapes are not just your ordinary tools. They're like magic seeds that, when combined and rearranged, can grow into fantastic, complex drawings! Picture this: you can transform a simple circle into a smiling sun or a square into a sturdy castle.

When you explore these shapes, you're not just improving your drawing skills; you're also nurturing your creativity. By mixing and matching, you can invent amazing designs you never thought possible! So, dive into the world of geometric shapes, young artists, and let your creativity soar! Who knows what extraordinary masterpieces you'll create?

DRAW CUBE

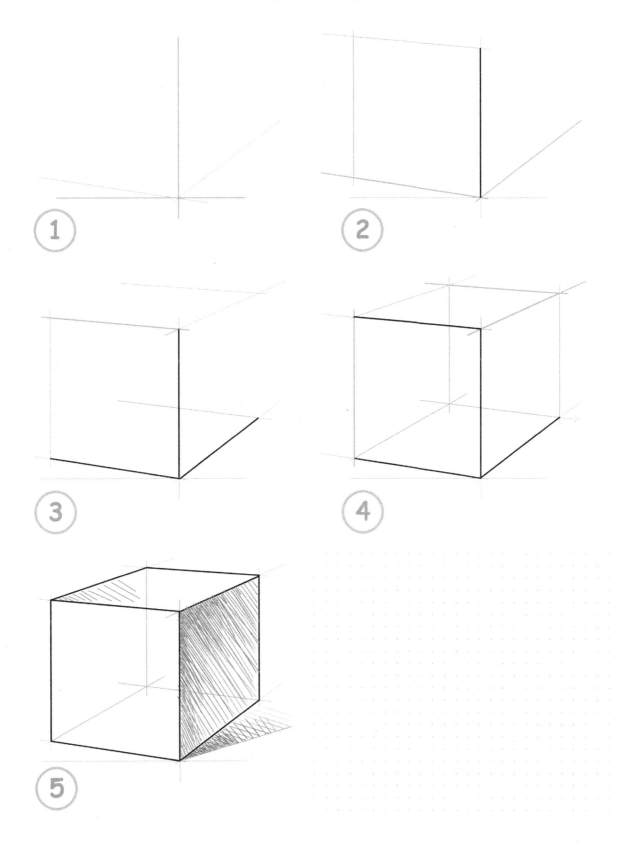

DRAW A BALL

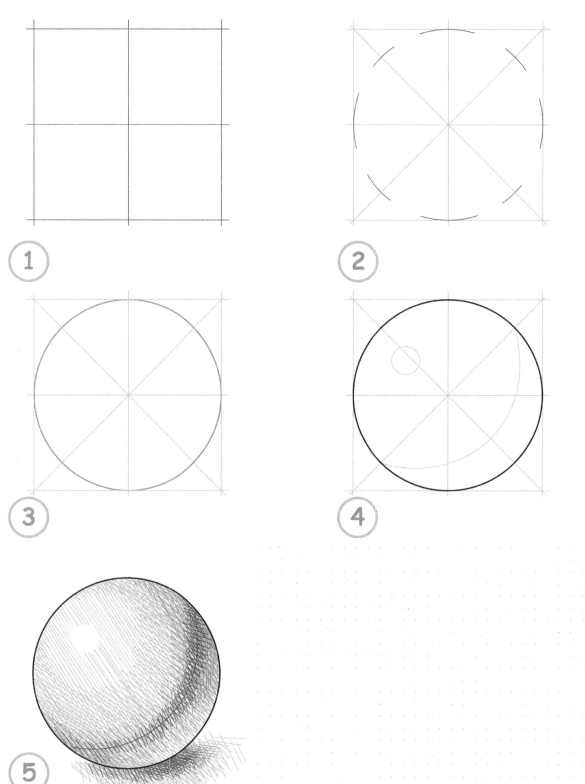

DRAW A CYLINDER

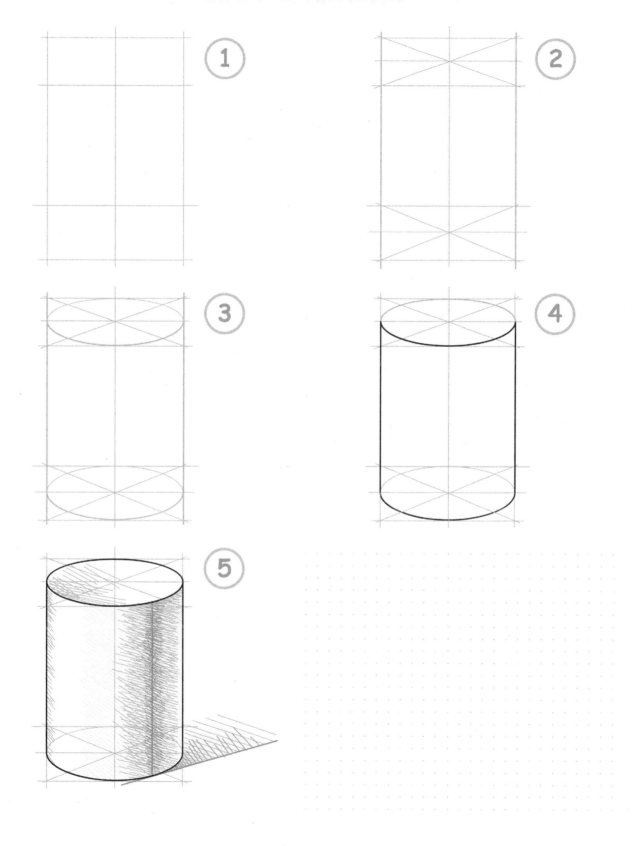

DRAW A CYLINDER AND CUBE.

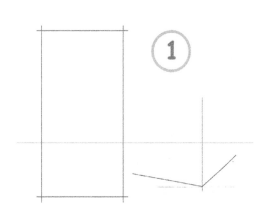

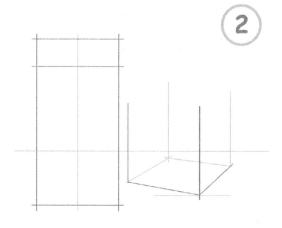

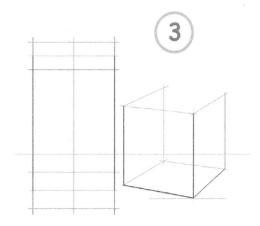

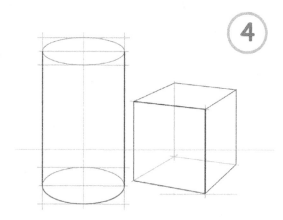

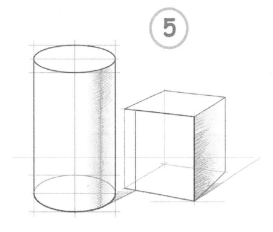

DRAW A BAL AND CUBE.

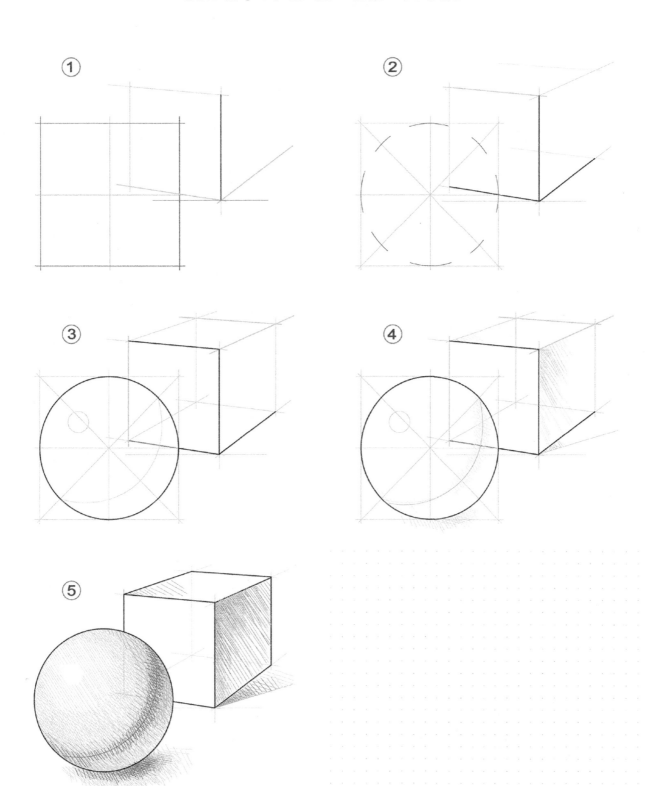

DRAW A STEP-WISE SKETCH

①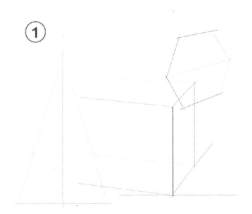

②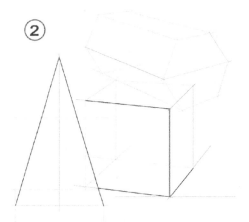

③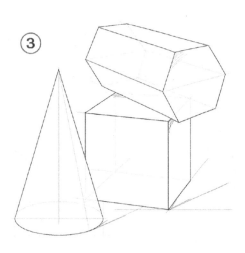

④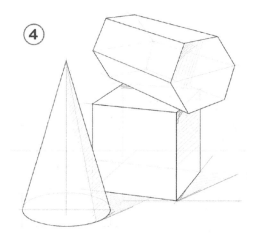

⑤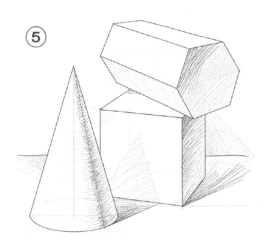

DRAW A PYRAMIDS

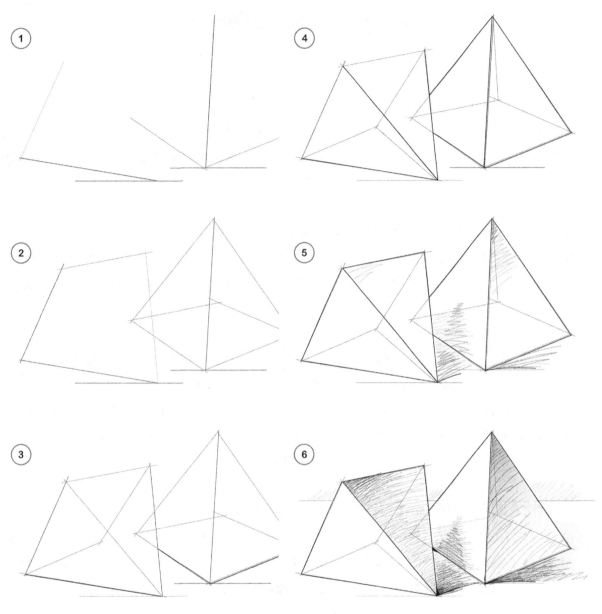

WELCOME TO THE EXCITING WORLD OF ANIME EYES!

DISCOVERING EMOTIONS: Have you ever noticed how anime eyes can speak volumes? They come in all shapes and sizes, helping artists like you showcase feelings in the coolest way possible. Mastering these expressive eyes adds a touch of magic to your characters, making them relatable and lively!

CHARACTER CHARM: Picture this - every anime character has a unique eye style. From sparkling eyes full of wonder to determined, focused gazes, each pair tells a story. Designing eyes for your characters is like giving them a personality makeover, making them memorable and one-of-a-kind.

STYLE THAT SPEAKS: Anime eyes aren't just eyes; they're a style statement! Imagine having the power to create eyes that fit seamlessly into your artwork, tying everything together in a fantastic, consistent style. Whether your characters are exploring distant lands or facing thrilling adventures, their eyes will captivate the audience, making them fall in love with your creations.

THE HEART OF ANIME ART: In the incredible world of anime, eyes are the heart and soul of every character. They convey dreams, hopes, and emotions, connecting the viewers to the story on a deep level. With each stroke of your pencil, you're not just drawing eyes; you're crafting a gateway to endless possibilities and unforgettable tales.

So, young artists, embrace this exciting challenge! Dive into the world of anime eyes, explore their myriad expressions, and watch your characters come to life in ways you've never imagined. Let your creativity soar, and let's embark on this amazing artistic journey together!

DRAW ANIME EYES

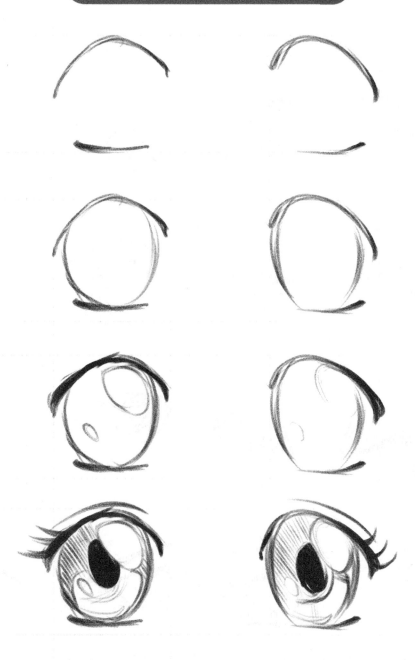

MASTERING ANIME EYES IS LIKE UNLOCKING A MAGICAL WORLD OF EMOTIONS! LEARN THE SECRETS OF DRAWING EXPRESSIVE AND CAPTIVATING ANIME EYES WITH SIMPLE, STEP-BY-STEP TECHNIQUES. DIVE INTO THE ART OF ADDING LIFE AND PERSONALITY TO YOUR CHARACTERS. LET YOUR IMAGINATION SOAR AS YOU CREATE EYES THAT TELL STORIES AND CONVEY FEELINGS. GET READY TO BRING YOUR ANIME CHARACTERS TO LIFE WITH EYES THAT SPARKLE AND SPEAK VOLUMES!

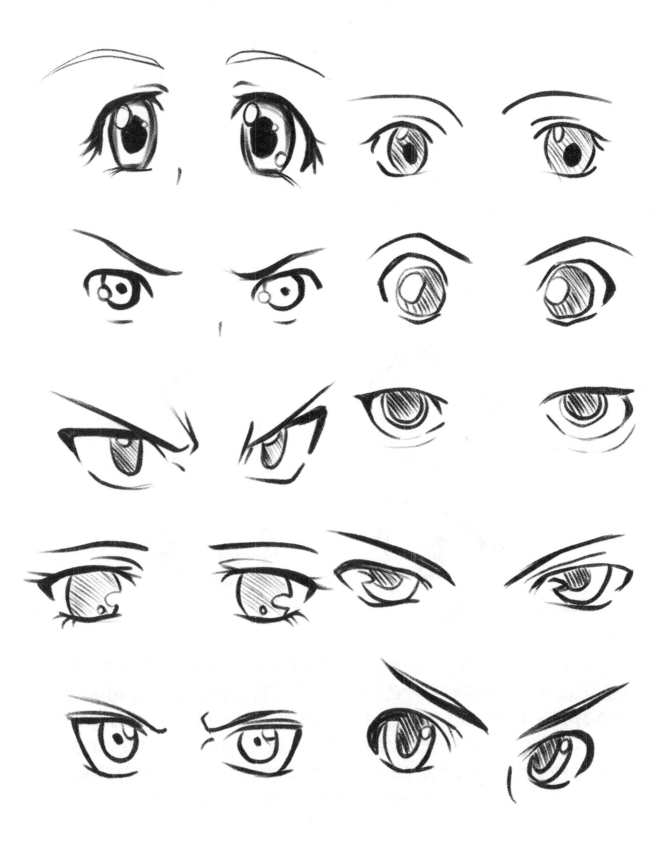

DRAW ANIME EYES

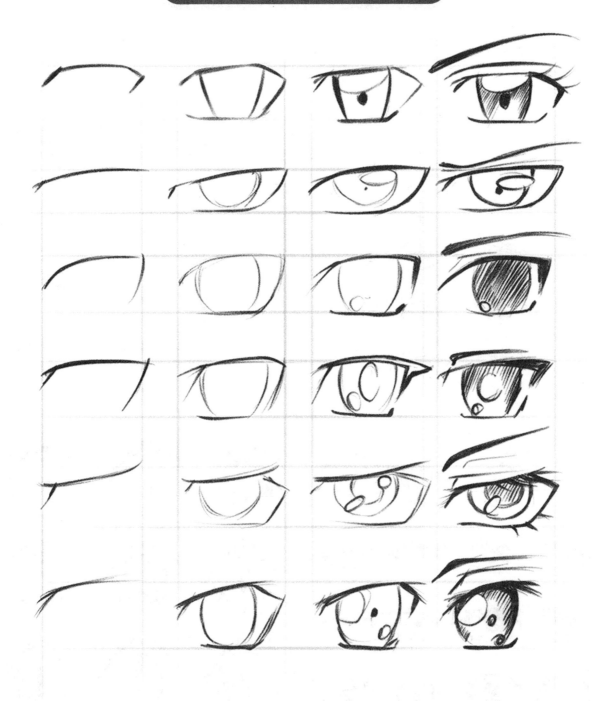

WHEN LEARNING TO DRAW ANIME EYES, FOCUS ON EXPRESSION AND DETAILS. PLAY WITH SIZES AND SHAPES TO CONVEY THE CHARACTER'S EMOTIONS. REMEMBER ABOUT LIGHTING AND REFLECTIONS THAT MAKE THE EYES COME ALIVE. EXPERIMENT AND DON'T BE AFRAID TO EXPRESS YOUR UNIQUENESS IN EVERY DETAIL!

DRAW ANIME EYES

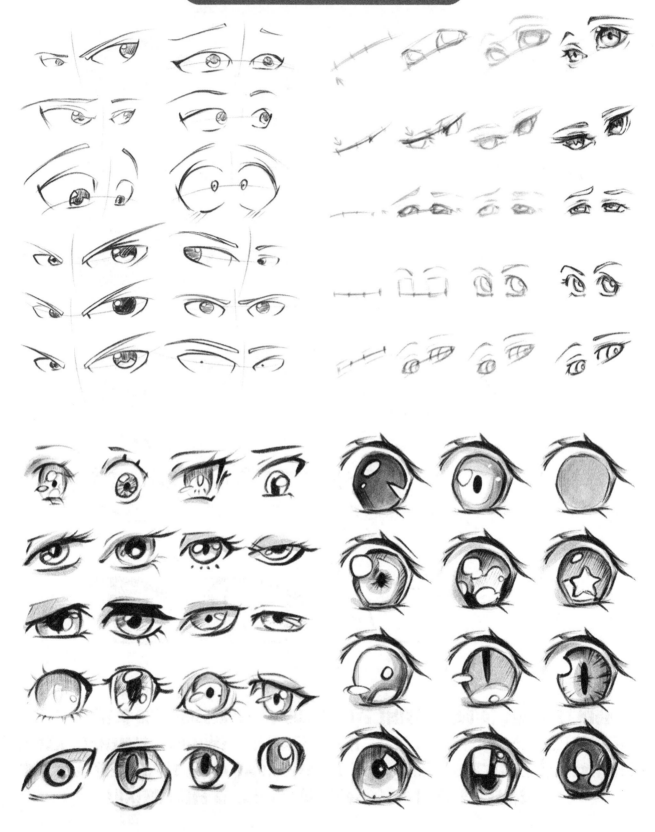

DRAW ANIME EYES

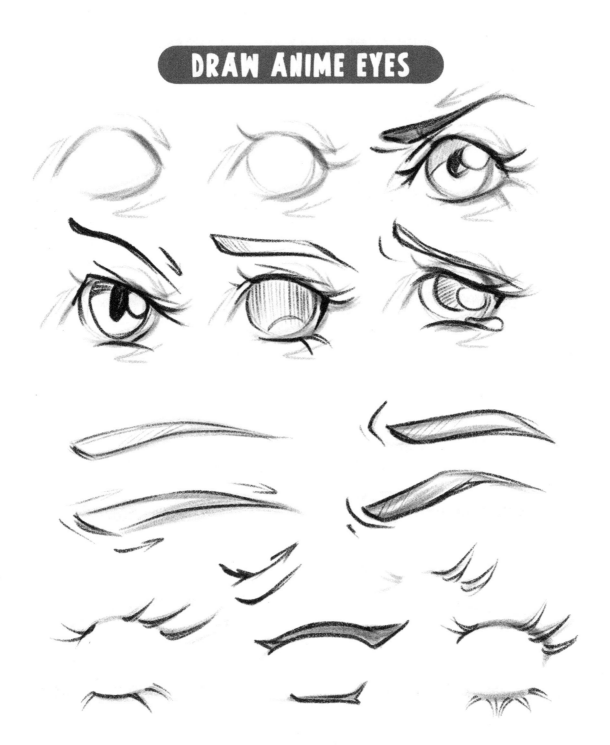

ADDITIONALLY, PAY ATTENTION TO THE EYEBROWS AND EYELASHES; THEY PLAY A SIGNIFICANT ROLE IN EXPRESSING EMOTIONS. PRACTICE CONSISTENCY AND SYMMETRY, BUT DON'T WORRY IF THEY AREN'T PERFECTLY IDENTICAL - IMPERFECTIONS CAN ADD CHARACTER. MOST IMPORTANTLY, HAVE FUN EXPERIMENTING WITH DIFFERENT STYLES AND EXPRESSIONS. YOUR CREATIVITY KNOWS NO LIMITS!

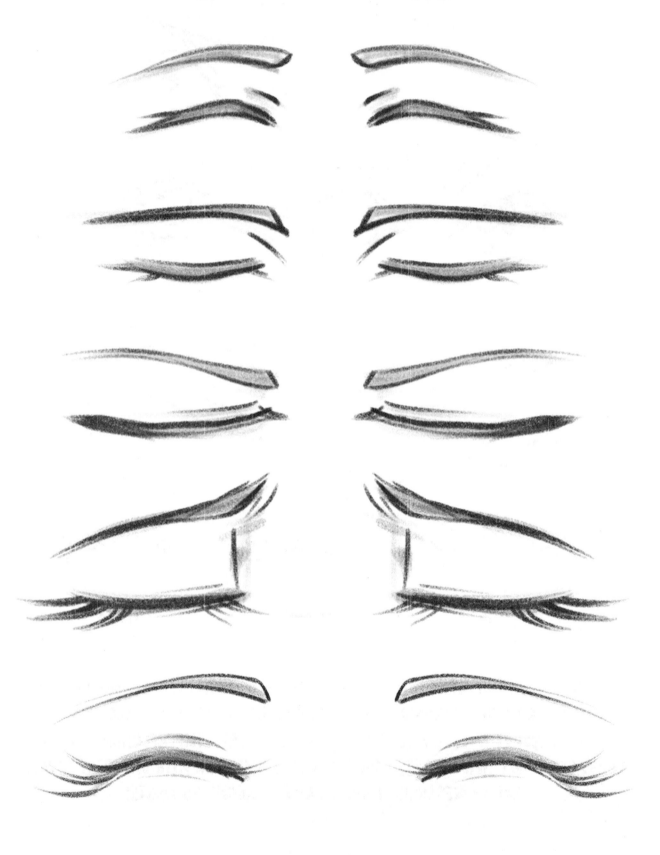

Let's Embark on the Exciting Journey of Drawing Anime Heads!

Begin With a Circle: Start your anime head by sketching a circle. This simple shape forms the foundation of your character's face.

Introduce a Cross: Draw a vertical line down the center of the circle and a horizontal line across it. This cross helps you position the eyes, nose, and mouth accurately.

Eyes and Nose: Anime eyes are often large and full of emotion. Place them along the horizontal line you drew earlier. Right below the eyes, add a small, cute nose. Keep it simple and sweet.

Mouth and Chin: Draw the mouth beneath the nose. Anime mouths are small and delicately curved. Then, create a soft, rounded chin just below the circle, connecting it seamlessly with the head.

Ears: Anime ears are typically simplified and start around the eyes, extending down to the nose level. Add them with gentle curves, making sure they complement the facial proportions.

Hair: Ah, the fun part! Anime hairstyles can be as creative as you like. Experiment with various styles - spiky, curly, straight - and let your imagination flow. Draw the hair around the head, considering its movement and volume. Anime characters often have unique and eye-catching hairdos.

Neck: Don't forget to include a slender neck beneath the head. It adds grace and realism to your character. The neck seamlessly connects to the shoulders, giving your anime creation a more natural appearance.

Express Yourself: Once you've mastered the basics, it's time to play with expressions! Try drawing your character with different emotions - happiness, sadness, surprise - and watch how their personality shines through.

Remember, practice is the key to improvement! The more you draw, the more confident you'll become in capturing the essence of anime characters. So, grab your pencils and let your creativity soar! Happy drawing!

DRAW ANIME HEADS

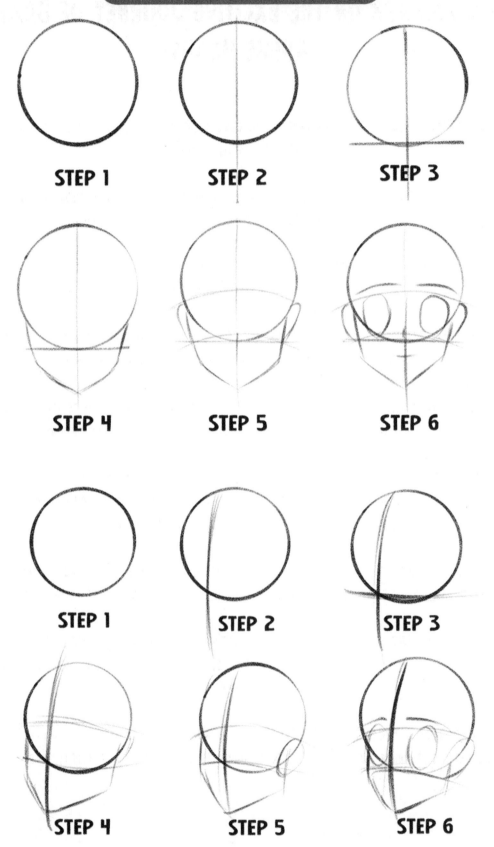

STEP 1   STEP 2   STEP 3

STEP 4   STEP 5   STEP 6

STEP 1   STEP 2   STEP 3

STEP 4   STEP 5   STEP 6

DRAW ANIME HEADS

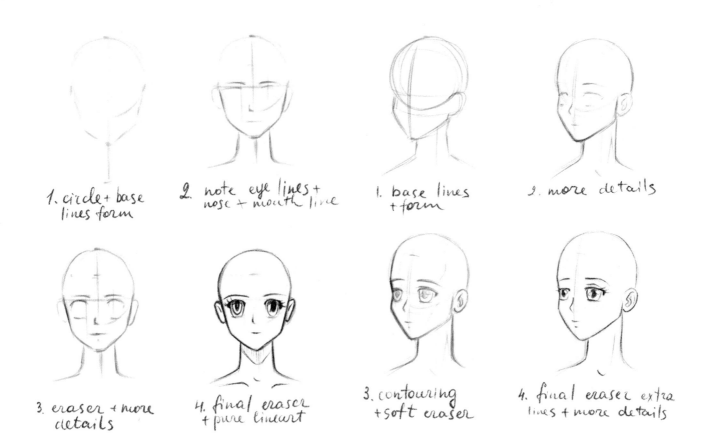

1. circle + base lines form

2. note eye lines + nose + mouth line

1. base lines + form

2. more details

3. eraser + more details

4. final eraser + pure lineart

3. contouring + soft eraser

4. final eraser extra lines + more details

WHEN DRAWING ANIME HEADS, FOCUS ON PROPORTIONS AND SYMMETRY. PAY ATTENTION TO THE PLACEMENT OF FACIAL FEATURES, LIKE EYES, NOSE, AND MOUTH. PRACTICE DIFFERENT ANGLES TO CAPTURE EXPRESSIONS ACCURATELY. DON'T FORGET TO EXPERIMENT WITH HAIR STYLES AND ACCESSORIES, AS THEY ADD PERSONALITY TO YOUR CHARACTERS. KEEP PRACTICING, AND REMEMBER, EVERY ARTIST HAS THEIR UNIQUE STYLE!

DRAW ANIME HEADS

1. draw circle + base forms

2. add form + mass for nose + mouth

1. base form head + neck

2. see where eye + nose line

3. soft wipe the sketch + let's contour

4. final wipe stitch + details

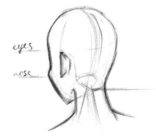

3. eye + nose lines helps build ear

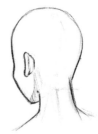

4. eraser + final lines

1. base circle + form like front face

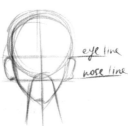

2. base lines eye + nose lines, note ears

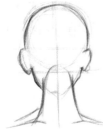

3. eraser lines, add more details

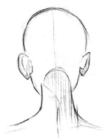

4. final eraser, final lines

DRAW ANIME HEADS

1. base circle

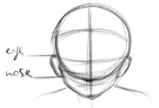

eye
nose

2. help lines   half circle

1. build circle-cylinder

2. draw help lines + form

3. soft eraser + details

4. final eraser + details lineart

3. eraser soft + more details

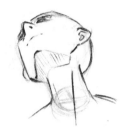

4. final eraser + finish details

LEARNING TO DRAW ANIME HEADS FROM DIFFERENT ANGLES AND SHAPES IS A CRUCIAL SKILL FOR EVERY ARTIST. IT NOT ONLY EXPANDS YOUR KNOWLEDGE AND CREATIVE POSSIBILITIES BUT ALSO MAKES YOUR CHARACTERS MORE INTERESTING AND UNIQUE. UNDERSTANDING HOW CHANGES IN PERSPECTIVE AND SHAPE AFFECT THE APPEARANCE OF THE HEAD ALLOWS YOU TO CREATE CHARACTERS WITH DIFFERENT PERSONALITIES AND EMOTIONS. THIS SKILL OPENS DOORS TO ENDLESS OPPORTUNITIES IN THE WORLD OF ANIME AND ENABLES YOU TO EXPRESS YOUR CREATIVITY AT A NEW LEVEL!

DRAW ANIME HEADS

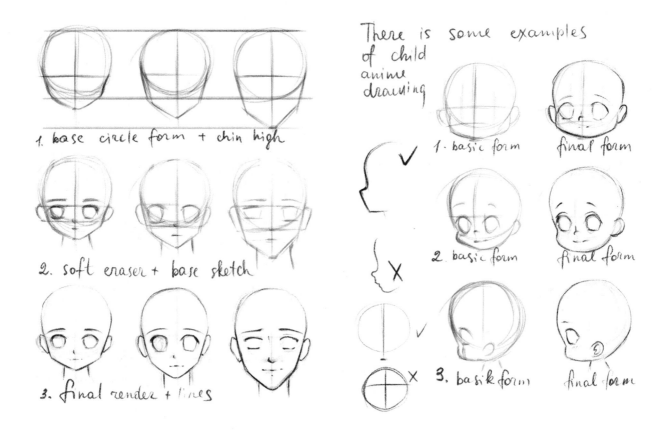

1. base circle form + chin high

2. soft eraser + base sketch

3. final render + lines

There is some examples of child anime drawing

1. basic form — final form

2. basic form — final form

3. basik form — final form

WHEN LEARNING TO DRAW A CHILD'S ANIME HEAD, IT'S ESSENTIAL TO START WITH THE BASICS. FOCUS ON UNDERSTANDING THE PROPORTIONS OF A CHILD'S FACE AND PRACTICE DRAWING DIFFERENT FACIAL EXPRESSIONS. PAY ATTENTION TO THE UNIQUE FEATURES LIKE BIG, EXPRESSIVE EYES AND INNOCENT SMILES THAT CAPTURE THE ESSENCE OF CHILDHOOD. PRACTICE REGULARLY, AND DON'T BE AFRAID TO MAKE MISTAKES. EACH MISTAKE IS A STEP TOWARD IMPROVEMENT. ADDITIONALLY, OBSERVE REAL-LIFE CHILDREN'S FACES AND STUDY HOW THEIR FEATURES DIFFER FROM ADULTS. INCORPORATE THOSE OBSERVATIONS INTO YOUR DRAWINGS, AND MOST IMPORTANTLY, HAVE FUN AND ENJOY THE CREATIVE PROCESS!

DRAW ANIME NOSES

WHEN DRAWING ANIME NOSES, ESPECIALLY FOR CHILDREN, IT'S CRUCIAL TO KEEP THEM SIMPLE AND IN HARMONY WITH THE OVERALL STYLE. HERE ARE SOME TIPS FOR KIDS LEARNING TO DRAW ANIME NOSES:

1. SIMPLICITY IS KEY: START WITH BASIC SHAPES. ANIME NOSES ARE OFTEN DRAWN AS SMALL DASHES OR DOTS. AVOID OVERLY COMPLICATED DETAILS.

2. PLACEMENT: PLACE THE NOSE SLIGHTLY ABOVE THE HALFWAY POINT BETWEEN THE EYES AND THE CHIN. FOR CHILDREN, KEEP THE NOSE HIGHER ON THE FACE FOR A YOUTHFUL LOOK.

3. EXPERIMENT WITH STYLES: ANIME OFFERS VARIOUS NOSE STYLES, FROM SIMPLE DOTS TO TINY HORIZONTAL LINES. ENCOURAGE KIDS TO EXPERIMENT AND FIND A STYLE THAT SUITS THE CHARACTER'S PERSONALITY.

4. CONSISTENCY IN SIZE: ENSURE THE SIZE OF THE NOSE IS CONSISTENT WITH THE CHARACTER'S AGE AND FACIAL PROPORTIONS. SMALLER NOSES ARE COMMON IN CHILD CHARACTERS.

5. PRACTICE FACIAL EXPRESSIONS: NOSES PLAY A CRUCIAL ROLE IN EXPRESSING EMOTIONS. PRACTICE DRAWING NOSES IN DIFFERENT ANGLES AND SHAPES TO CONVEY VARIOUS EXPRESSIONS.

6. OBSERVE REAL FACES: STUDYING REAL NOSES, ESPECIALLY THOSE OF CHILDREN, CAN PROVIDE VALUABLE INSIGHTS. ENCOURAGE KIDS TO OBSERVE AND INCORPORATE THESE OBSERVATIONS INTO THEIR DRAWINGS.

7. PATIENCE AND PRACTICE: LEARNING TO DRAW NOSES, LIKE ANY OTHER SKILL, TAKES PRACTICE. ENCOURAGE CHILDREN TO BE PATIENT WITH THEMSELVES AND KEEP PRACTICING TO IMPROVE THEIR TECHNIQUES.

REMEMBER, EACH ARTIST DEVELOPS THEIR UNIQUE STYLE, SO IT'S ESSENTIAL TO EXPERIMENT AND FIND WHAT WORKS BEST FOR THEIR CREATIVE EXPRESSION

DRAW ANIME NOSES

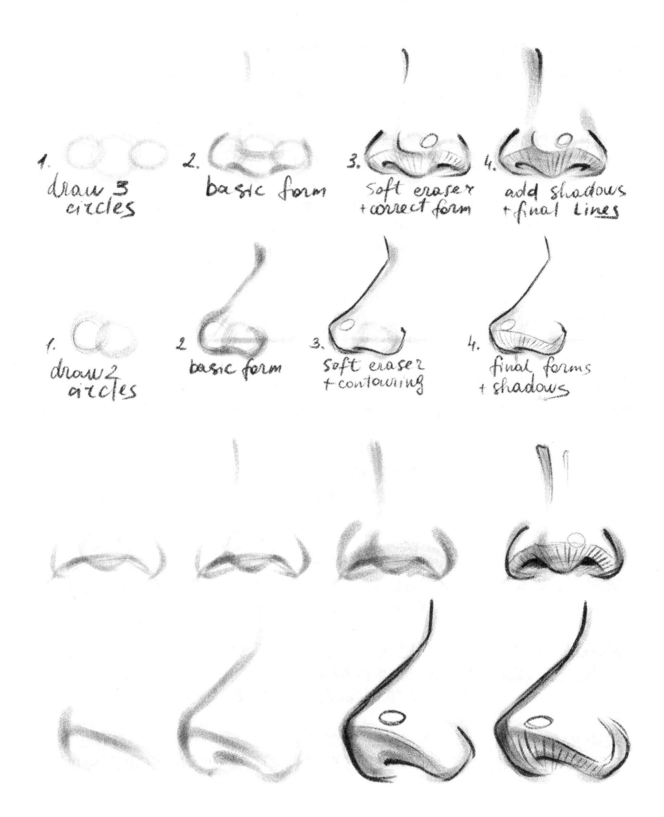

1. draw 3 circles

2. basic form

3. soft eraser + correct form

4. add shadows + final lines

1. draw 2 circles

2. basic form

3. soft eraser + contouring

4. final forms + shadows

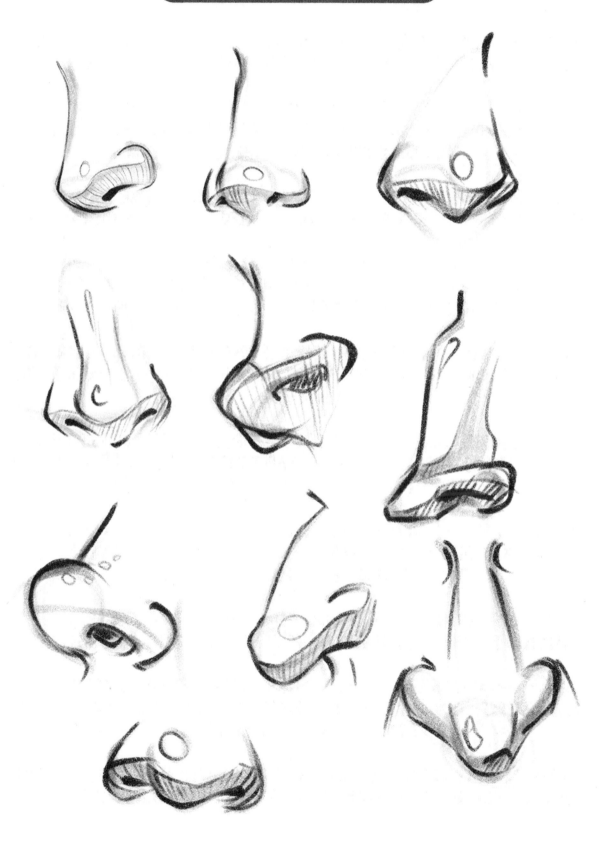

DRAW ANIME EARS

WHEN DRAWING ANIME EARS, ATTENTION TO DETAIL AND PROPORTION IS CRUCIAL. HERE ARE SOME TIPS FOR CHILDREN LEARNING TO DRAW ANIME EARS:

1. POSITIONING: PLACE THE EARS APPROXIMATELY BETWEEN THE EYEBROWS AND THE BOTTOM OF THE NOSE. FOR ANIME CHARACTERS, EARS ARE OFTEN SIMPLIFIED, SO KEEPING THEM SMALLER AND HIGHER ON THE HEAD IS COMMON.

2. BASIC SHAPES: EARS CAN BE SIMPLIFIED INTO BASIC SHAPES LIKE OVALS OR CIRCLES. START WITH THESE SHAPES AND THEN ADD SMALLER DETAILS LIKE THE EAR CANAL.

3. STUDY REAL EARS: ENCOURAGE KIDS TO OBSERVE REAL EARS, BOTH HUMAN AND ANIMAL, TO UNDERSTAND THE BASIC STRUCTURE. THIS OBSERVATION CAN HELP IN CREATING MORE REALISTIC AND VARIED EAR SHAPES IN ANIME DRAWINGS.

4. HAIR PLACEMENT: IF THE CHARACTER HAS LONG HAIR, ENSURE THE EARS ARE PARTIALLY HIDDEN BY THE HAIR STRANDS. THIS ADDS A NATURAL TOUCH TO THE DRAWING.

5. DETAILING: WHILE ANIME-STYLE EARS ARE SIMPLIFIED, ADDING A HINT OF THE EARLOBE OR THE CURVATURE INSIDE THE EAR CAN ENHANCE THE OVERALL LOOK. HOWEVER, AVOID OVERLY INTRICATE DETAILS, ESPECIALLY FOR YOUNGER CHARACTERS.

6. CONSISTENT STYLE: MAINTAIN CONSISTENCY IN THE STYLE OF EARS THROUGHOUT THE ARTWORK. IF THE CHARACTER HAS A SPECIFIC EAR SHAPE, ENSURE IT REMAINS CONSISTENT IN ALL PANELS OR ILLUSTRATIONS.

7. PRACTICE EXPRESSIONS: EARS CAN CONVEY EMOTIONS TOO. PRACTICE DRAWING EARS IN DIFFERENT POSITIONS AND ANGLES TO DEPICT VARIOUS EXPRESSIONS EFFECTIVELY.

8. EXPERIMENT WITH STYLES: ANIME OFFERS DIVERSE EAR STYLES, ESPECIALLY IN FANTASY GENRES. ENCOURAGE KIDS TO EXPLORE DIFFERENT ANIME SERIES TO SEE HOW ARTISTS INTERPRET EARS UNIQUELY.

REMEMBER, PRACTICE AND PATIENCE ARE KEY. WITH CONSISTENT PRACTICE, CHILDREN CAN IMPROVE THEIR ANIME EAR-DRAWING SKILLS AND DEVELOP THEIR ARTISTIC STYLE.

DRAW ANIME EARS

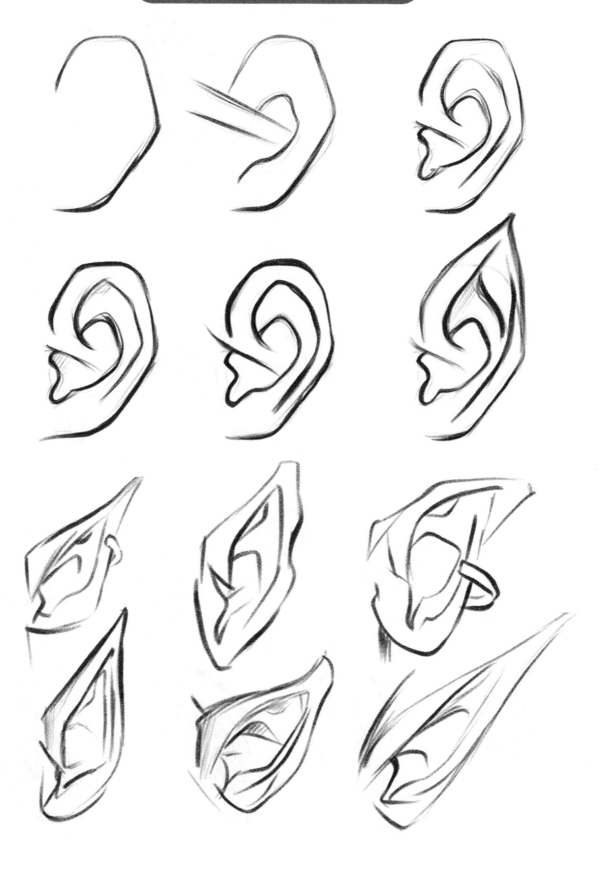

DRAW ANIME EARS

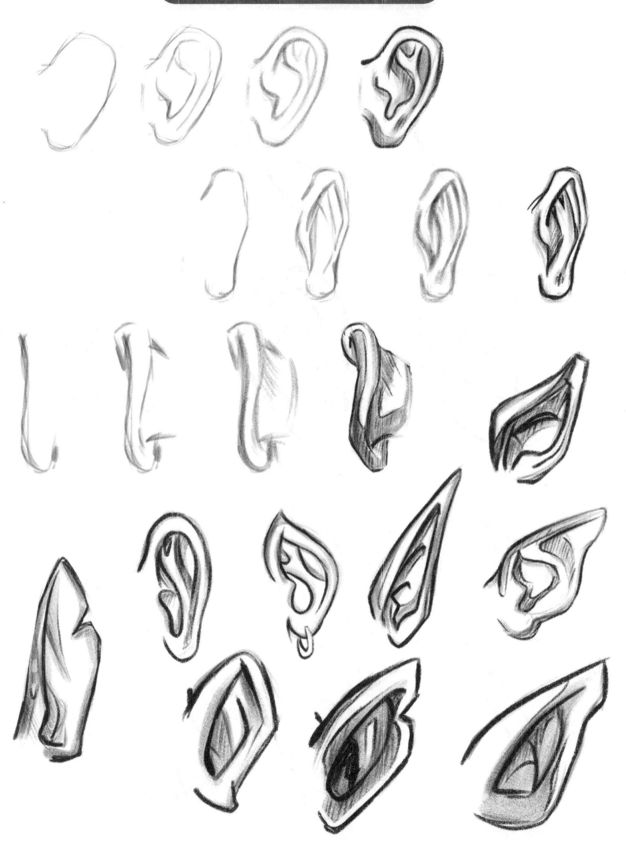

DRAW ANIME LIMBS

WHEN DRAWING ANIME LIMBS LIKE HANDS AND LEGS, ATTENTION TO PROPORTION AND ANATOMY IS ESSENTIAL. HERE ARE SOME TIPS FOR CHILDREN LEARNING TO DRAW ANIME LIMBS:

1. BASIC SHAPES: START WITH BASIC SHAPES LIKE CIRCLES AND OVALS FOR JOINTS. FOR HANDS, AN OPEN OVAL CAN REPRESENT THE PALM, AND SMALLER OVALS CAN DEPICT FINGERS. FOR LEGS, USE CYLINDERS FOR THIGHS AND SHINS.

2. PROPORTION: PAY ATTENTION TO THE PROPORTIONS OF LIMBS IN RELATION TO THE REST OF THE BODY. ANIME CHARACTERS OFTEN HAVE ELONGATED LIMBS, SO EXAGGERATE THE LENGTH SLIGHTLY FOR A MORE ANIME-STYLE LOOK.

3. HAND DETAILS: TO DRAW ANIME HANDS, START WITH A RECTANGULAR SHAPE FOR THE PALM AND ADD SMALLER RECTANGLES FOR FINGERS. REMEMBER THAT ANIME HANDS ARE OFTEN SIMPLIFIED, SO FOCUS ON BASIC SHAPES AND AVOID EXCESSIVE DETAILING.

4. LEG PLACEMENT: LEGS SHOULD BE POSITIONED IN A WAY THAT SHOWS BALANCE AND MOVEMENT. PRACTICE DRAWING LEGS IN VARIOUS POSES TO UNDERSTAND HOW BALANCE AFFECTS THE STANCE.

5. FEET SHAPES: FOR ANIME FEET, BEGIN WITH A SIMPLE SHAPE LIKE A WEDGE. ADD CURVES TO REPRESENT TOES WITHOUT EXCESSIVE DETAIL. STUDY DIFFERENT SHOE STYLES IN ANIME TO ADD VARIETY TO YOUR DRAWINGS.

6. GESTURE AND MOVEMENT: ANIME LIMBS OFTEN CONVEY EMOTION AND MOVEMENT. PAY ATTENTION TO THE GESTURE OF HANDS AND LEGS; THEY SHOULD ALIGN WITH THE CHARACTER'S EXPRESSION AND POSE.

7. STUDY ANATOMY: WHILE ANIME STYLE ALLOWS FOR SIMPLIFICATION, HAVING A BASIC UNDERSTANDING OF HUMAN ANATOMY, ESPECIALLY FOR HANDS, CAN GREATLY IMPROVE THE QUALITY OF DRAWINGS. STUDY REAL HANDS AND LEGS TO GRASP THEIR STRUCTURE.

8. PRACTICE EXPRESSIONS: HANDS CAN CONVEY EMOTIONS TOO. PRACTICE DRAWING HANDS AND LEGS IN VARIOUS GESTURES TO DEPICT DIFFERENT EXPRESSIONS AND MOVEMENTS ACCURATELY.

9. CONSISTENT STYLE: MAINTAIN A CONSISTENT STYLE THROUGHOUT YOUR ARTWORK. IF YOU CHOOSE A SPECIFIC HAND OR LEG STYLE, ENSURE IT REMAINS UNIFORM IN ALL YOUR DRAWINGS.

REMEMBER, PRACTICE IS KEY TO IMPROVEMENT. ENCOURAGE KIDS TO DRAW HANDS AND LEGS IN DIFFERENT POSES AND SITUATIONS, AS THIS HELPS ENHANCE THEIR SKILLS AND CREATIVITY.

DRAW ANIME LIMBS

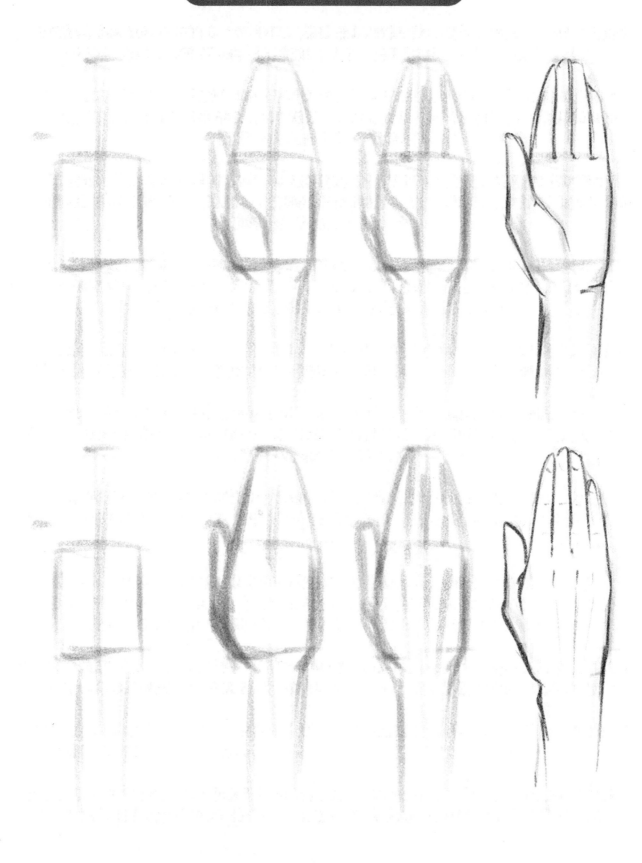

DRAW ANIME LIMBS

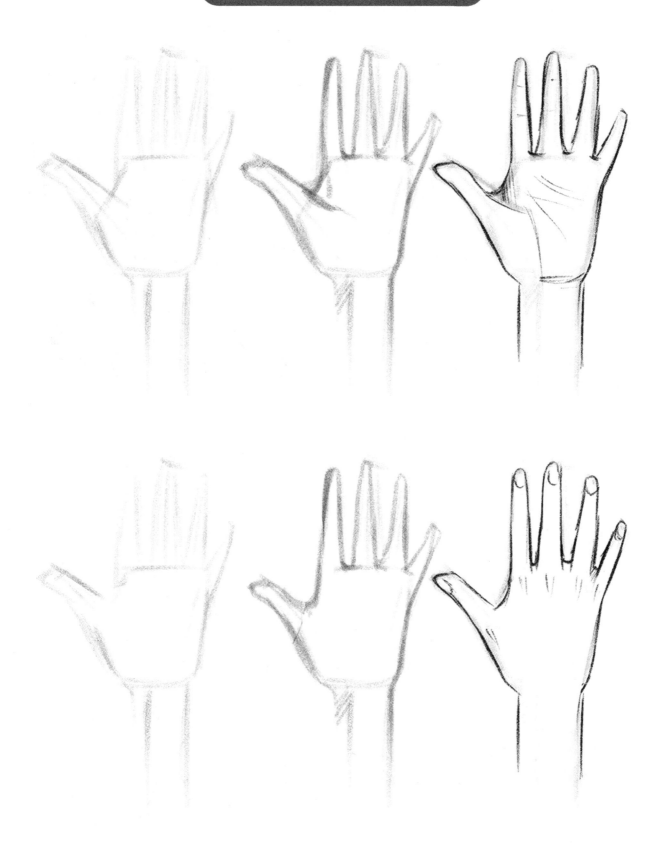

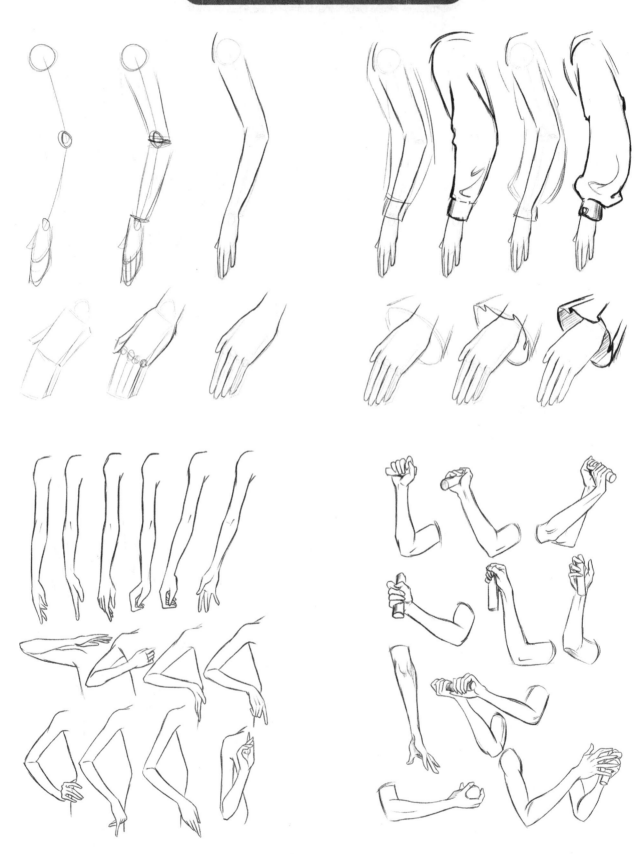

DRAW ANIME LIMBS

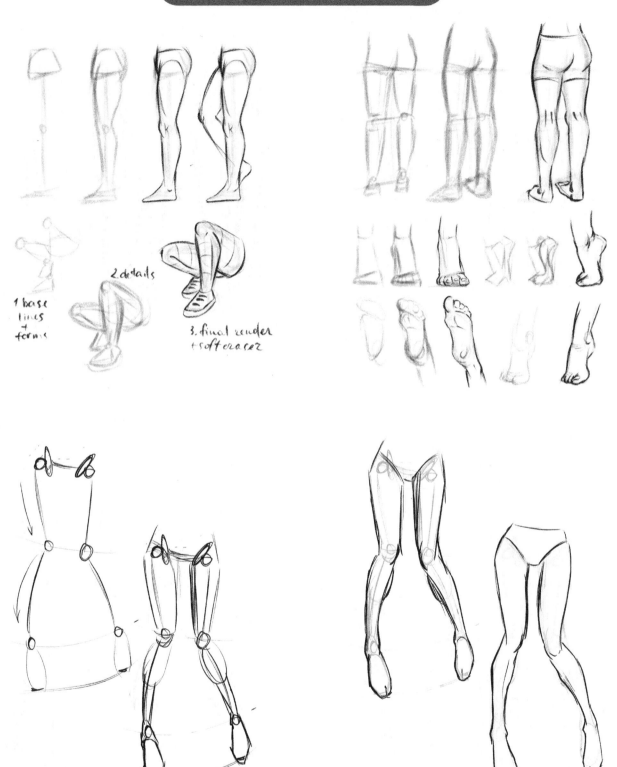

1 base lines + forms

2 details

3. final render + soft eraser

DRAW ANIME LIMBS

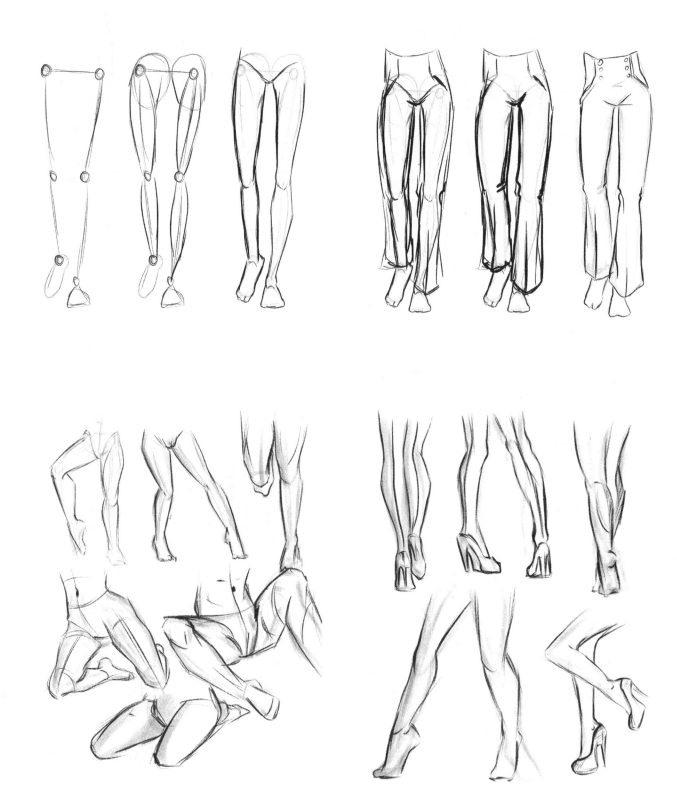

DRAW ANIME EMOTIONS

WHEN CAPTURING EMOTIONS IN ANIME CHARACTERS, IT'S ESSENTIAL TO FOCUS ON FACIAL EXPRESSIONS AND BODY LANGUAGE. HERE ARE SOME TIPS FOR CHILDREN LEARNING TO DRAW ANIME EMOTIONS:

1. FACIAL FEATURES: ANIME CHARACTERS OFTEN HAVE LARGE, EXPRESSIVE EYES. EXPERIMENT WITH EYE SHAPES, SIZES, AND POSITIONS TO CONVEY DIFFERENT EMOTIONS. FOR EXAMPLE, WIDE-OPEN EYES CAN INDICATE SURPRISE, WHILE NARROWED EYES CAN SHOW DETERMINATION.

2. MOUTH EXPRESSIONS: THE MOUTH PLAYS A CRUCIAL ROLE IN CONVEYING EMOTIONS. EXPERIMENT WITH DIFFERENT MOUTH SHAPES, INCLUDING SMILES, FROWNS, AND OPEN OR CLOSED MOUTHS. THE POSITION OF THE MOUTH CORNERS CAN INFLUENCE THE EMOTION BEING PORTRAYED.

3. EYEBROWS: ANIME EYEBROWS ARE QUITE EXPRESSIVE. VARY THE EYEBROW SHAPE AND POSITION TO REFLECT DIFFERENT EMOTIONS. RAISED EYEBROWS CAN INDICATE SURPRISE OR CURIOSITY, WHILE DOWNWARD-SLOPING EYEBROWS CAN DEPICT SADNESS OR ANGER.

4. BODY LANGUAGE: EMOTIONS ARE NOT JUST ABOUT FACIAL EXPRESSIONS. PAY ATTENTION TO THE CHARACTER'S POSTURE, GESTURES, AND

5. USE OF COLOR: COLOR

6. PRACTICE EXPRESSIONS: ENCOURAGE KIDS TO PRACTICE DRAWING

7. OBSERVE REAL EMOTIONS: ENCOURAGE CHILDREN TO

8. EXPERIMENT WITH STYLES: ANIME ALLOWS FOR A WIDE RANGE OF ARTISTIC STYLES. ENCOURAGE CHILDREN TO EXPERIMENT WITH DIFFERENT ANIME STYLES TO FIND THE ONE THAT BEST SUITS THE EMOTION THEY WANT TO CONVEY. SOME STYLES MAY EMPHASIZE EXAGGERATED FEATURES, WHILE OTHERS FOCUS ON SUBTLE EXPRESSIONS.

9. TELL A STORY: ENCOURAGE KIDS TO CREATE A STORY OR CONTEXT FOR THE CHARACTER THEY ARE DRAWING. UNDERSTANDING THE CHARACTER'S BACKGROUND AND SITUATION CAN HELP THEM DEPICT EMOTIONS MORE ACCURATELY.

REMEMBER, PRACTICE AND OBSERVATION ARE KEY. BY OBSERVING REAL-LIFE EMOTIONS AND PRACTICING DIFFERENT EXPRESSIONS, CHILDREN CAN ENHANCE THEIR ABILITY TO CONVEY EMOTIONS EFFECTIVELY IN THEIR ANIME DRAWINGS.

DRAW ANIME EMOTIONS

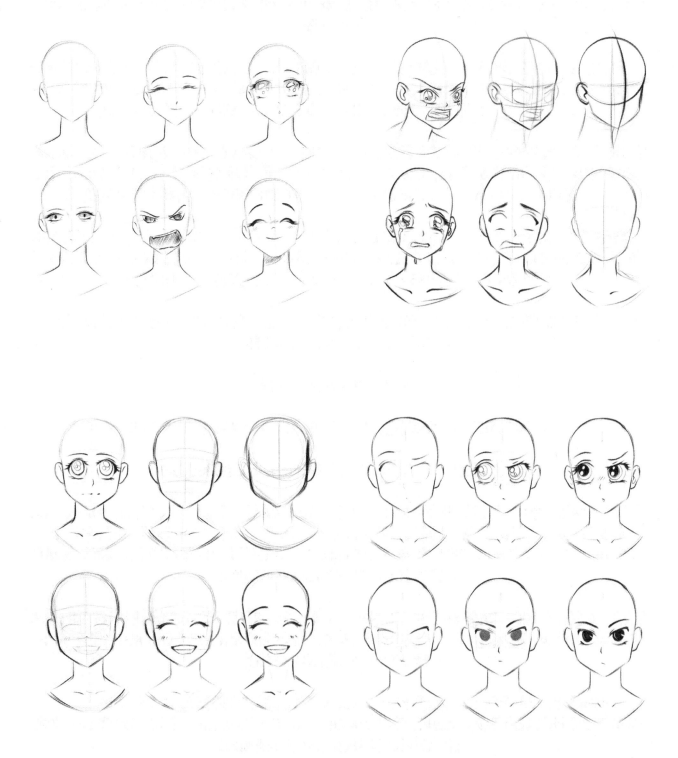

DRAW ANIME EMOTIONS

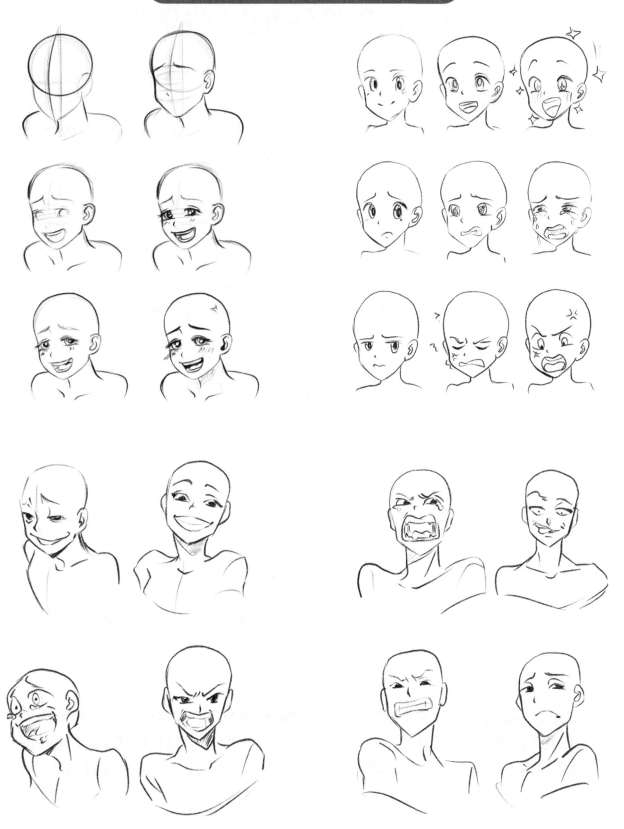

LET'S MASTER DRAWING ANIME HAIR!

FLOW AND DIRECTION: Anime hair often has dynamic flow and direction. Pay attention to the direction of the strands. Are they blowing in the wind, falling naturally, or spiked up? Understanding the flow adds life to your character's hairstyle.

SIMPLE SHAPES: Break down complex hairstyles into basic shapes. For example, think of a ponytail as a cylinder and long hair as flowing ribbons. Start with these shapes and add details gradually.

LAYERS AND VOLUME: Anime hair has layers, giving it volume and depth. Use curved lines to create layers, making the hair look more realistic. Thick, bold lines can be used for outlining, while thinner lines add texture.

BANGS AND FRINGES: Pay attention to the style of bangs or fringes. They can be straight, wavy, or spikey. Bangs often cover part of the forehead and curve naturally around the face.

ACCESSORIES: Anime characters often wear hair accessories like bows, clips, or headbands. These accessories can complement the hairstyle and add a touch of personality to your character.

SHADING AND HIGHLIGHTS: Use shading to create depth and highlights to add shine. Lightly shade areas where shadows fall, and leave some parts untouched for highlights. This technique gives the hair a realistic and glossy appearance.

PRACTICE DIFFERENT STYLES: Anime offers a wide range of hairstyles, from short and spiky to long and flowing. Practice drawing various styles to expand your skills and versatility.

REMEMBER, PRACTICE MAKES PERFECT! EXPERIMENT WITH DIFFERENT SHAPES, STYLES, AND LENGTHS TO CREATE UNIQUE AND EYE-CATCHING ANIME HAIRSTYLES. WITH EACH DRAWING, YOU'LL ENHANCE YOUR SKILLS AND BRING YOUR CHARACTERS TO LIFE. HAPPY DRAWING!

DRAW ANIME HAIR

DRAW ANIME HAIR

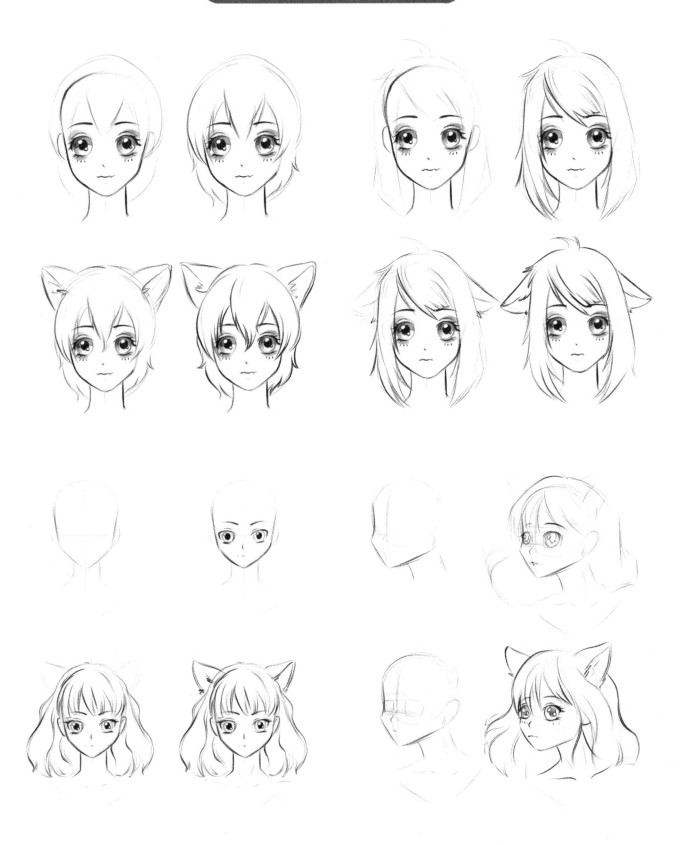

79

DRAW ANIME HAIR

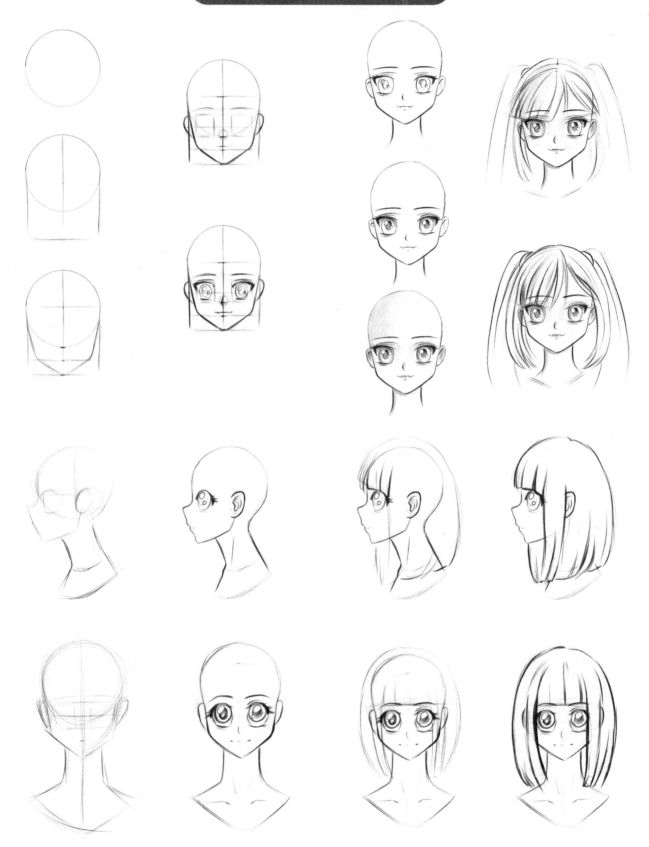

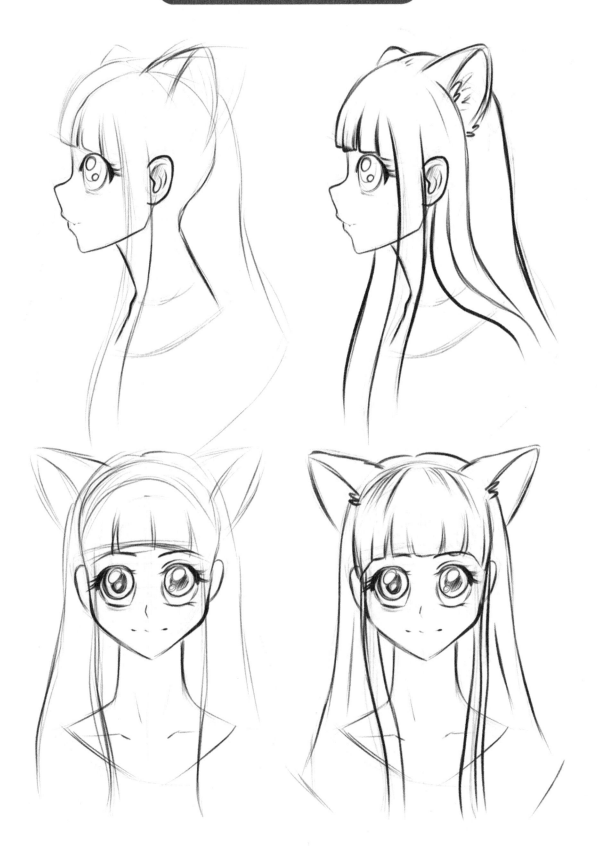

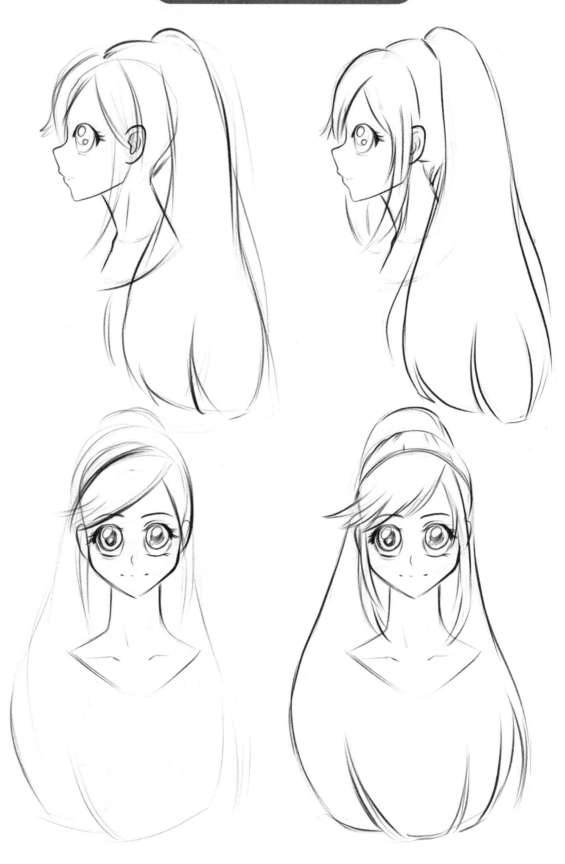

WELCOME TO THE NEXT EXCITING CHAPTER!

NOW THAT YOU'VE MASTERED DRAWING INDIVIDUAL PARTS OF ANIME CHARACTERS, IT'S TIME TO LEVEL UP! GET READY TO DIVE INTO A MORE CHALLENGING REALM. WE'RE STEPPING INTO THE WORLD OF DRAWING COMPLETE ANIME CHARACTERS, BOTH IN STILL POSES AND IN MOTION.

ARE YOU EXCITED? IN THIS CHAPTER, WE'LL EXPLORE THE MAGIC OF BRINGING YOUR CHARACTERS TO LIFE - CAPTURING THEM IN MOMENTS OF STILLNESS AND IN THE MIDST OF ACTION. GET YOUR PENCILS READY, YOUNG ARTISTS, BECAUSE WE'RE ABOUT TO EMBARK ON AN AMAZING ARTISTIC ADVENTURE TOGETHER!

DRAW ANIME CHARACHERS

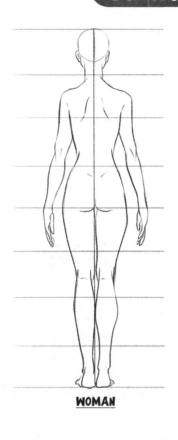

WOMAN

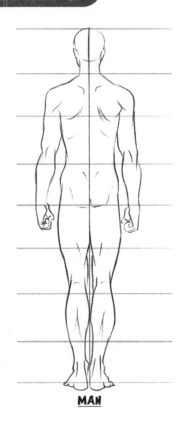

MAN

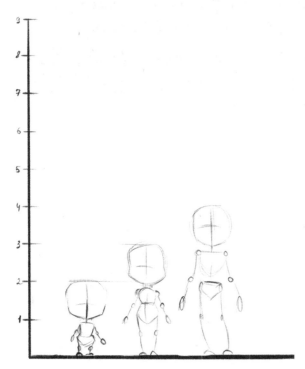

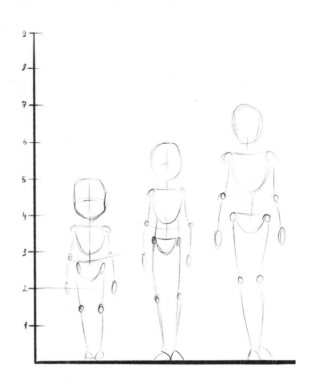

DRAW ANIME CHARACHERS

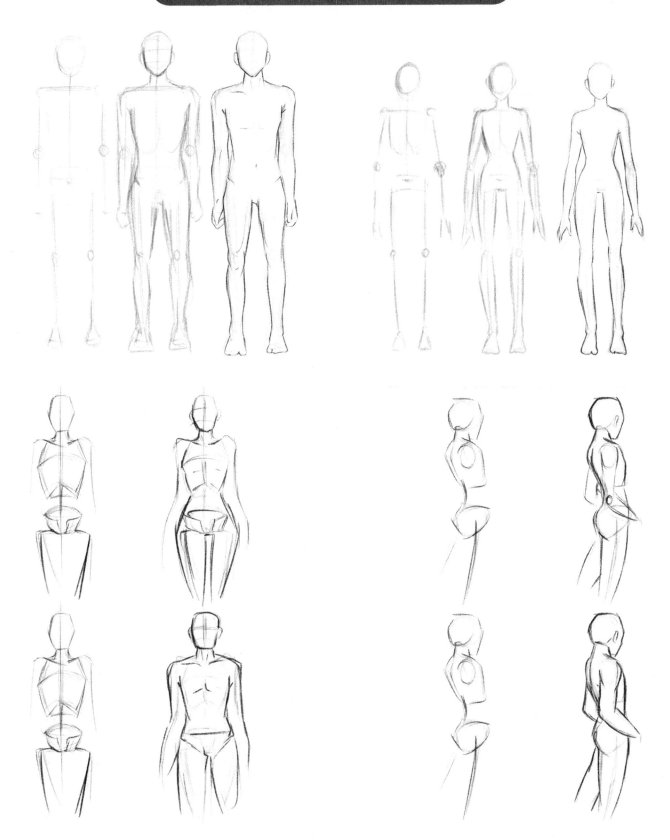

DRAW ANIME CHARACHERS

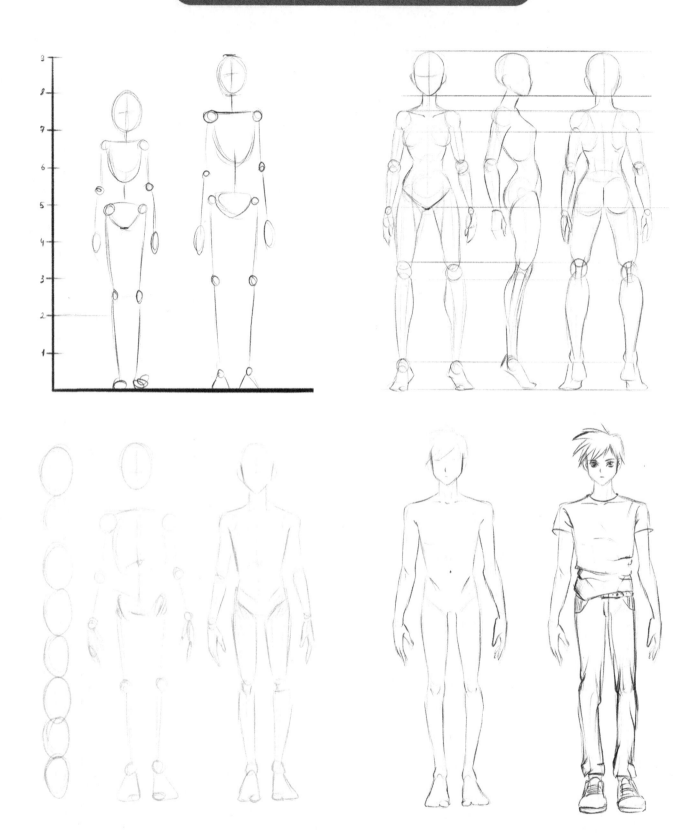

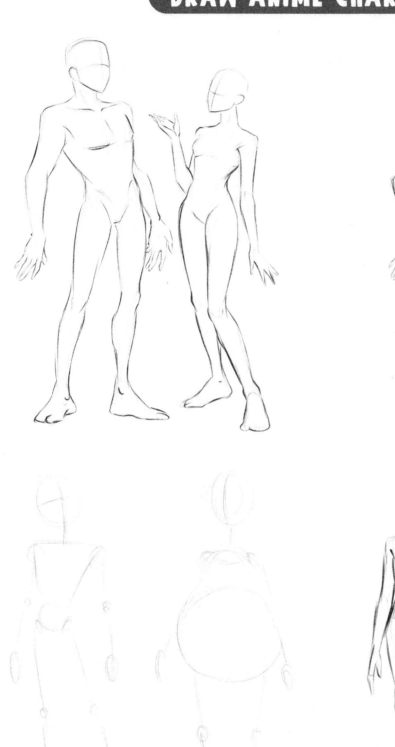

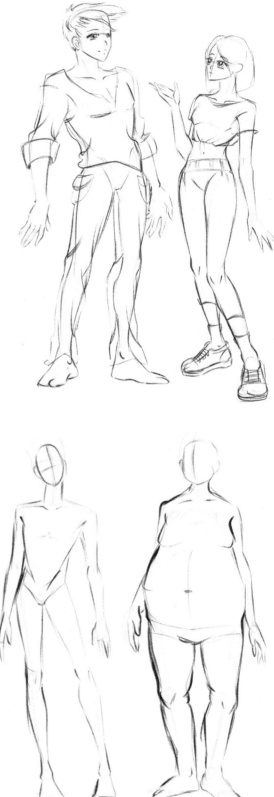

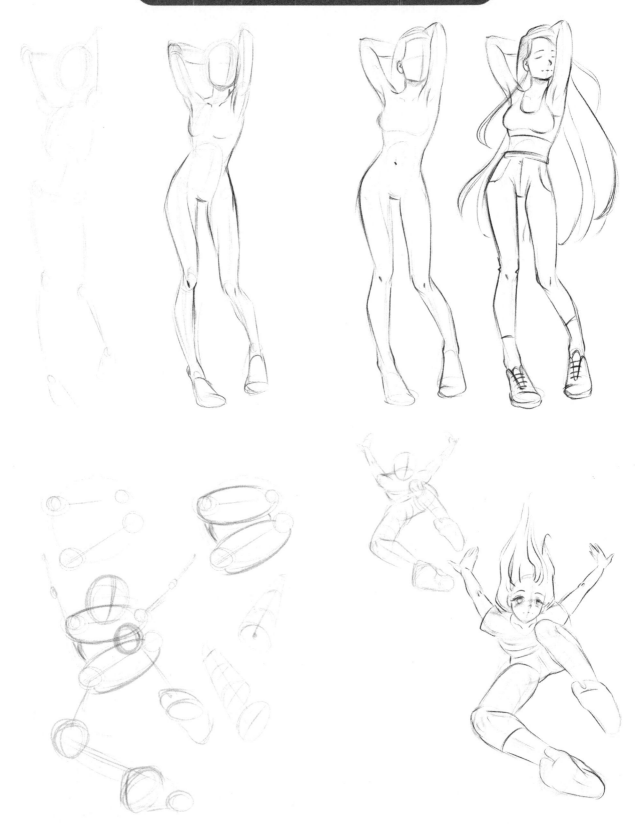

DRAW ANIME CHARACHERS

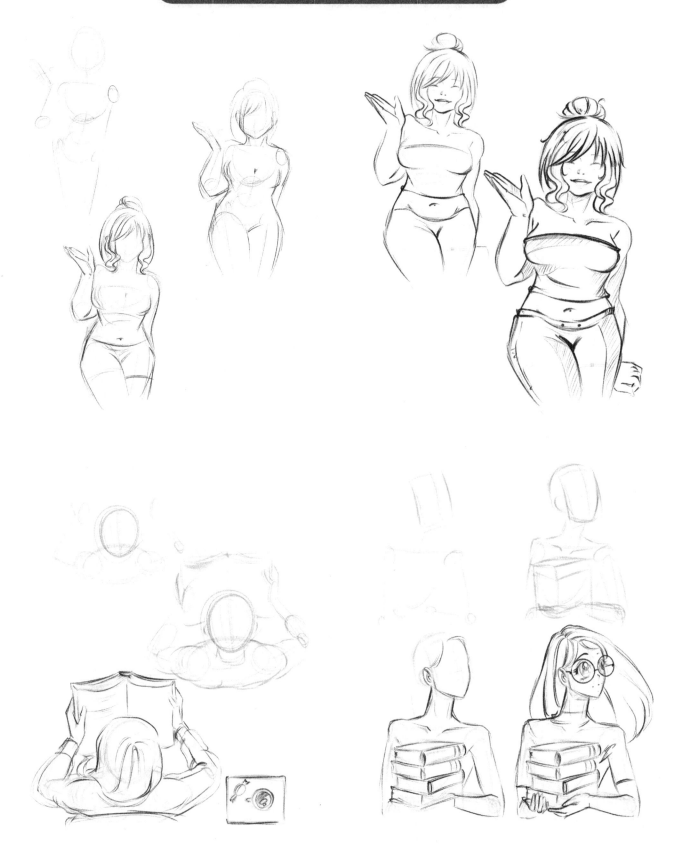

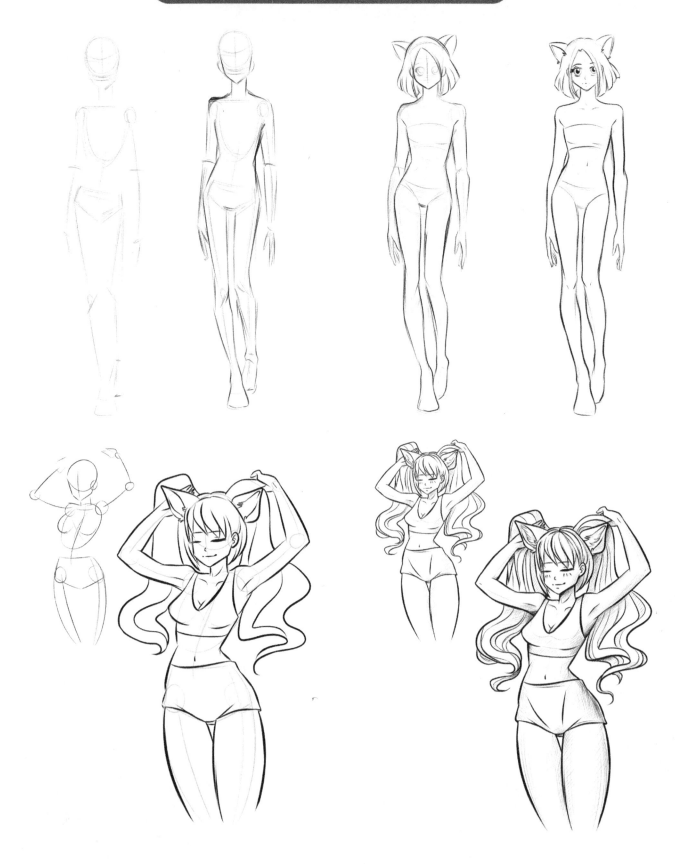

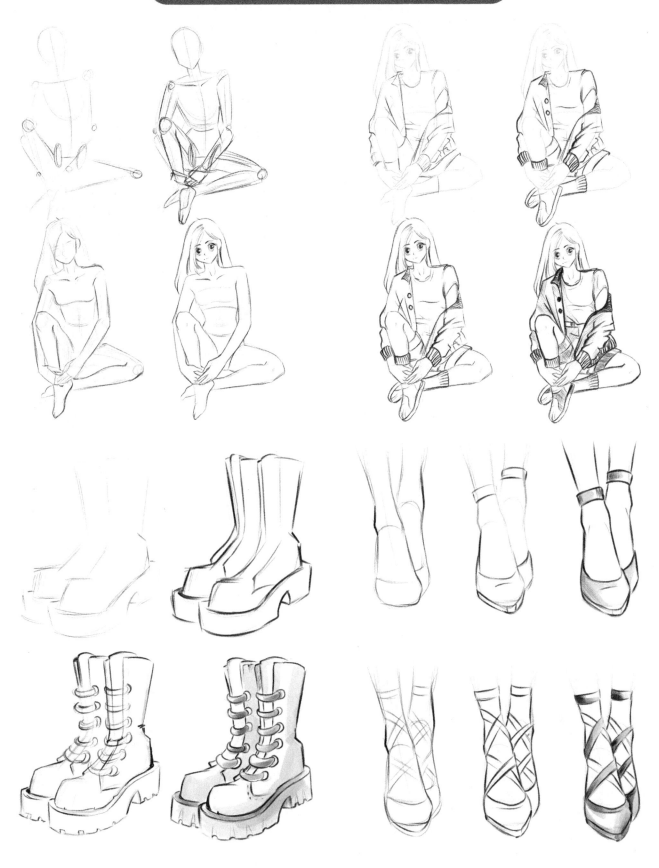

97

DEAR READER,

I want to express my heartfelt gratitude for choosing to bring my anime drawing book into your creative world. Your support means the world to me. I sincerely hope that the techniques and tips shared within these pages inspire your artistic journey and bring your anime creations to life in the most magical way.

Thank you for trusting in my guidance. Happy drawing, and may your imagination soar to new heights!

Warm Regards,

PATRICIA ROGERS

Made in the USA
Las Vegas, NV
01 December 2024

13044095R00057